Can I Trust You With My Money?

The Little Book Of Financial Wizardry

Noreen Gonce

BookPartners, Inc.
Wilsonville, Oregon

Although the author and publisher have researched all sources to ensure the accuracy and completeness of the information contained in this book, we assume no responsibility for errors, inaccuracies, omissions or any other inconsistency herein. Any slights against people or organizations are unintentional. Readers should consult an attorney or accountant for specific application to their situation.

Copyright 1997 by Noreen Gonce
All rights reserved
Printed in U.S.A.
Library of Congress Catalog 96-83860
ISBN 1-885221-40-1

This book may not be reproduced in whole or in part, by electronic or any other means which exists or may yet be developed, without permission of:

BookPartners, Inc.
P.O. Box 922
Wilsonville, Oregon 97070

Dedication

To my sister, without whose question, "How can I find a financial advisor?" this book would not have happened;

To my mother, without whose words of, "You can do it," I would not have tried; and

To my husband, without whose cooking we would have gotten very thin. I dedicate these pages.

Acknowledgments

Acknowledgment for their great assistance goes
to my colleagues who shared stories,
to my clients who shared dreams and
to the attorneys who shared horror stories.
The form of this book was greatly influenced
by you all. Thank you.

Table of Contents

	Introduction 1
1	If You're a Widow There's a Bullseye on Your Back 7
2	Would You Give Your Money to a Stranger? ... 19
3	Ignorance is *Not* Bliss 29
4	Your Odds of Outwitting Your Broker Are About as Good as Winning the Lottery 35
5	Romancing the Investment 45
6	Blowing Smoke in Your Advisor's Face is Dangerous to Your Wealth 53
7	How to Lose Your Shirt with "Shortcut" Reports 59
8	Trusting Your Hunch 65
9	Deceptions and Distortions: Con Games People Play 71
10	Can I Trust You with My Money? Or, Is That Rock For Real? 79
11	Unsuitable, Inappropriate and Unfit 89
12	What's Wrong With Chasing Yesterday's Winner? 97
13	There Are No Free Lunches — or Seminars .. 105
14	Follow-the-Leader Investing Can Take You Right Over the Cliff 117

15	Bending the Truth About Mutual Funds	123
16	Prenuptial and Cohabitation Agreements: Before You Jump In with Both Feet	137
17	Is My Broker in Love with Me or My Money?	147
18	Seeing Through the Funhouse Mirror	153
19	Choosing as if Your Retirement Depends on It	161
20	Prohibited Acts, Or Is Someone Pulling a Fast One?	167
21	SEC and Associations Information	171
22	What's In a Title?	179

Introduction

Americans are financially illiterate.

And, even more frightening, they are indifferent to their lack of investor knowledge, which makes them "pigeons" for fast-talking stockbrokers.

A 1996 survey by the Investor Protection Trust of Arlington, Virginia, revealed that in the richest country in the world less than twenty percent of its citizens understand financial matters specifically related to investing. Less than one-third of them have ever drawn up a specific financial plan, even though such a plan is the foundation on which all financial decisions should be based, including buying a house, and funding college or retirement.

There is still a gender gap when it comes to investments. Only about eleven percent of the women in America are investment literate, compared to about twenty-five percent of the men. There is also an age gap; nearly half of the over-sixty-five group fell into the least-knowledgeable category. Although younger investors seem to know more about how to invest money, nearly one-third are woefully lacking!

Answers to eight basic questions by nearly two-thirds of those polled showed basic ignorance about mutual fund charges. A majority believed that mutual funds charge no sales or any other fees. More than three-fifths did not know that bond prices fluctuate inversely to interest rates. Nearly half did not know that the purpose of diversification is to reduce risk. The same uninformed fifty percent did not understand the protection provided by the Securities Investor Protection Corporation.

I see the results of investor ignorance and indifference in my clients as they struggle to build secure futures. It's in their faces when I have to tell them they don't have enough assets to fund their dreams—they must reduce their retirement lifestyle expectations or work a few years longer to increase their portfolio.

Introduction — 3 —

Answers to the survey I've cited provide the reason I've written *Can I Trust You With My Money?* It's because only about ten percent of those illiterate, indifferent people who do get professional advice ever check on the disciplinary record of their broker or planner! That's like waiting for an accident to happen.

In the years of my practice I have consulted with many different money-attitude types. There are people who compulsively spend, and those who are just as compulsive about saving. There are those who think money is an evil necessity, and those who just don't think about it at all. There are those who are so afraid of investing they compensate by maintaining rigid control of their money, and there are those whose passion is more, more more! It is a challenge to identify the best way to work with each and a satisfaction to watch them succeed.

I've written this little book as a quick-reading source of basic information about choosing a broker or planner. All of the stories are true, though I've changed all the names to protect the innocent who still must face their friends, and the guilty who still must make a living. Many of the stories are humorous; others demonstrate the gullibility and misplaced trust of investors. All of them are presented as information to help the reader to exercise caution when he or she makes a decision to entrust money with an "expert."

Good luck!

Introduction

Can I Trust You With My Money?

What is it about money?
    It brings out the best in us...and the worst.
People lie for it...steal it...hoard it.
    They earn it...squander it...give it away.
Families are created...and destroyed;
    Countries make...and break alliances.
It's a measure of success...and of failure.

Money causes more relationship problems than sex.
We don't understand how it works,
    Yet there are few classes teaching it.
Religions have attitudes about it;
    Psychotherapists see patients over it.
It's hard to live with it
    And impossible to live without it.

– Noreen Gonce

1 If You're a Widow There's a Bullseye on Your Back

"The number one target victim in the United States is widows. There's a belief that widows are very elderly. You know, of course, that the average age of a widow in America is fifty-six years!"

Jason, a staff member at the regional Association of Retired Persons (AARP) office, paused to let his words sink in. His feet propped on a utilitarian desk, he cradled a beige phone in the bend of his shoulder and neck.

"According to our surveys and the complaints from our members, it's the widows who are in jeopardy," he emphasized.

"Really?! I didn't realize that!" replied Corbin. He was the man on the other end of the line to whom Jason was talking. A financial planner, he was engaged in research for a talk at the senior center about appropriate retirement investments. Corbin had been in practice more than ten years and was known for his casual style and easy way of providing answers. His buttery voice was often heard on radio and in seminars.

"Yes," Jason said, "widows are prime targets for schemers ranging from the old 'Let me repair your aluminum siding' to 'Your recently-departed husband ordered this leather bound Bible with your name embossed in gold but he didn't pay for it and it's COD.' We don't get too much of the Bible ploy anymore. Now it's more in car and home repairs. And stock investments."

Before Corbin could respond, Jason added, "Insurance is another area in which problems occur. An agent delivers death proceeds to a grieving widow, points out how wonderful it is that her husband provided this little windfall, and convinces her to take a policy out on herself on behalf of her children. Of course, the premium takes a lot of the death benefit he just delivered. He sells her by getting her to focus on how grateful her children will be. Completely takes her mind off the fact that she needs the money to pay debts or for income.

"We just got involved in a case on behalf of one of our members. It seems that Miranda — that's not her name — has been receiving calls for several years from a young man at a small brokerage firm. Miranda is in her early eighties and has a not-so-modest portfolio with a large brokerage. This man wants her to move it to him.

"Miranda was very sharp in managing her and her husband's accounts, but she's getting forgetful and fuzzy in her thinking. She lives alone, has no close family, and only a few of the friends she and her husband shared are still living. She doesn't drive, so she is a virtual recluse except for walking to the grocery store.

"According to the story Miranda told us, this is what happened to her:

"At first the phone calls she received from the young stockbroker were all business, but over a period of months they turned into little chats. She started looking forward to talking to Bob Smith (that's what we'll call him), discussing the news and things like that. He was real nice, so respectful. He always asked if he was interrupting anything. Miranda talked to his assistant also, when Bob got called away by an important client. She was a friendly young woman, and the two of them talked girl things.

"They were like my best friends," Miranda said. "It was almost as if I had family again. They'd just call and pass the time of the day. Valentine's Day came and I got a heart-shaped box of chocolates — nice ones, not the cheap dimestore kind. I was so surprised!" She was so touched at being remembered that she sat down and cried. Mother's Day came and she got an orchid — not a corsage; it was a plant with three purple and white blooms on a long curving stem! Her birthday came and she received yellow roses, her most favorite-in-all-the-world kind. Her husband, bless his soul, used to give them to her for special occasions.

"Bob Smith or his female assistant would mention an investment or two while they were talking with Miranda. Nothing ever pushy, just a comment about how good it was doing or how he'd just heard it was going to take off. He never asked Miranda to buy anything after those first few calls. 'We were just friends,' she said, 'and they were sharing how their day was going.'

"Then Miranda got really sick, and her landlady called one of those agencies for the elderly for assistance. The court sent someone to help her with her personal affairs. What that means is that the agency woman took over Miranda's checkbook and her investments. She went through all of Miranda's papers, trying to get them organized.

"One thing led to another after the woman spotted the checks Miranda had sent to that nice young man, Bob Smith, for investments. She took Miranda's statements to have someone look at them.

"Anyway," said Miranda, "the whole thing turned out to be a lie! The promises Smith had been telling me about how many people were making money — it was all a lie. I lost a lot of money. She — the lady from the court — went down there and saw the manager. He said I ordered those things on my own, that the broker had never asked me to buy. She shot right back that I wouldn't have known about them if Bob Smith hadn't told me and, besides, I was a gullible, lonely old lady.

"They tell me that my broker will be fined," Miranda said, "but it's still unclear whether he'll have to reimburse me. I wouldn't be a very good witness because of my poor memory, so it would be such a relief if he voluntarily paid it back."

Corbin, the broker who was preparing a senior center talk about retirement investments, was silent on the other end of the line. He was thinking about his wife and his own mother, wondering how vulnerable they might be one day.

Older widows, especially those who've had a long traditional marriage in which husbands, attorneys, bankers and brokers — males, all — made the financial decisions, are prone to continue their dependence on the male gender. Unfortunately, their assumption of good intentions and honesty from their advisors, combined with their naiveté about financial matters, makes them sitting ducks for those who put their own interests first. Three other widow horror stories illustrate how nasty the game becomes.

A recently widowed eighty-year-old had been a homemaker her entire life. She did volunteer work, participated in church activities, and raised her children. Her assets consisted of a $65,000 mobile home, $20,000 in clothes, jewelry, furniture, etc., and a $150,000 securities portfolio.

Her broker, who knew she was overwhelmed by the thought of making her own financial decisions, offered to help her by "taking care of everything."

In thirteen months he made 140 trades for her. She realized a loss of $65,000, and the broker earned $29,000 in commissions. This level of trading activity was unsuitable for an elderly widow with limited resources who needed income! It's unsuitable for anyone!

In the second case, the aged victim was eighty-five years old and could not even remember her own name. She had three accounts, each with a different broker. One account was personal, one was an estate account, and the last was a joint account with her two sons. The total of the three amounted to one million dollars, all of which was invested in municipal bonds and CDs (Certificates of Deposit).

In three years there were 600 trades in her accounts, causing a loss of $345,000. Her brokers earned $161,000 in gross commissions.

Unsuitable? You bet! She was very elderly, had absolutely no experience in the stock market, and besides had enough assets to provide her with an income without taking the risk of stocks. In addition, given her failing mental condition, she probably needed a conservator, which means her brokers were on thin ice for dealing with her at all.

However, don't think it's always strangers who take advantage of widows. They are targeted as well by members of their own families! Their motives? Greed?

Running over someone who is in the way? Misguided good intentions? Probably a bit of each. Look what happened to Samantha:

"Oh, no! I wouldn't dream of signing any of my assets over to my children! Not after what happened to my friend Samantha!" Abigail, outraged, nearly came across her attorney's desk. Her pale blue eyes, normally calm and serene, were a fireworks of alarm. "I, I — no, I just couldn't do it."

She slumped back into her chair, nervously smoothing the folds in her soft pink dress. The desk light caught the glitter of her antique diamond rings and ornately jeweled watch.

"It's okay, Abigail," soothed Kendall, her attorney. "It was only one way of handling things. We can do something else."

Kendall has been Abigail's attorney for many years. They had grown old together, and she respected his advice, usually taking it. She had never had such a violent reaction to his recommendations.

"Obviously something bad must have happened to Samantha," he said. "Would you like to tell me about it?"

Abigail looked at her old friend and saw the concern in his brown eyes. She realized time was passing relentlessly for both of them when she noted the gray in his red eyebrows and handlebar mustache.

   She sighed and said, "Samantha is my friend from Ladies' Golf. She never had a lot of money, but she had enough. She was worried about protecting her assets in case she was mentally incapacitated. Also, she was concerned about being able to pay for nursing-home care. Her mother had Alzheimer's, you know, and spent her last years in a nursing home. Someone suggested she put the bulk of her money in her married daughter's name. That way she'd have a "back-up" account with a younger person as a signer who could manage it if she couldn't. It seemed like the perfect solution. She told me she'd talked with her daughter about retitling the account, and her daughter agreed it would be all right.

   "This happened a year or so ago. Just recently Samantha was faced with horrendous medical bills from tests her doctors ran when she had that pain and dizziness. Thankfully, she's going to be fine. Anyway, she told her daughter she would need some of her reserve money to finish paying the bills. Her daughter told her the money was gone! They used it to remodel their kitchen!! Samantha told me how beautiful their new kitchen was when they were redoing it, but I know she didn't have the slightest idea it was done with her money. What a shock!

"Samantha has really struggled since then. The hardest thing for her is knowing she has no cushion in case of an emergency. She can't very well sell a kitchen cabinet to raise money!"

A Bit of Financial Wizardry

Women who have never managed their finances need an advocate when they are widowed. That advocate should walk with them as they learn, be a sounding board, and be available for counseling at all meetings having to do with finances (including those involving charitable gifting). An advocate acts as a wise consultant but does not make final decisions.

When a widow is mentally diminished, a conservator should be appointed as soon as possible. That, in itself, could cause a family row if family factions are vying for control. A durable power of attorney having been executed prior to the onset of diminished capacity is the best solution.

A widow who has participated in financial decisions with her husband must learn to do it on her

If You're a Widow There's a Bullseye On Your Back   – 17 –

own. Again, an advocate is a big help. Also, there are classes, seminars and books with lots of good information. The best advice for a new widow is, don't buy yet!

Young or old, experienced in financial matters or not, the new widow should postpone all investment decisions for at least six months, preferably a year, until a sense of proportion returns after the grieving period.

Do not sell the house, move far away, change brokers, or make radical changes in anything for a year. It will take that long to think straight again. Some widows describe it as "coming out of a fog."

Get a new will drafted as soon as possible. It can be changed later if necessary.

Run, do not walk, to your attorney if anyone, including family members, tries to scare you or your widowed friend into signing documents you or she do not understand.

2
Would You Give Your Money to a Stranger?

"The March meeting of the Penny Benders Association will come to order, please." The solid thwack of a mahogany gavel striking the sounding block silences the murmuring voices.

"I couldn't help overhearing part of your conversation," said Joanne, the president. "Maybe we should share as many experiences as we can about problems with stockbrokers. We're nearly ready to make our first purchase as an investment club, and we'll need to select a broker before we can do that. Annie, would you like to share?"

Annie squirmed in her wooden chair and fidgeted with her purse strap. She was in her late twenties, with red hair that fell in waves onto the shoulders of her dark blue middle-management suit. Normally outgoing, she was weighing whether to share an embarrassing moment. Then she began to speak softly.

"Well, as some of you already know, I inherited a little bit of money from my mother. I promised myself to use it for investing, and I would begin before I turned thirty. I interviewed several different stockbrokers to find someone with whom I felt comfortable. Most were referred by attorneys at my firm, and a couple had ads in the paper for seminars. I finally found Sandra. She was easy to talk to and seemed real knowledgeable.

"I told her I wanted to start with $10,000, and she made several recommendations. We met a couple times before I was ready to take the plunge. Then, when the time came, I could hardly think, much less concentrate. That caused our meeting to run longer than we planned. Finally it was time to write the check, and I asked who I should make it out to. There we were, sitting at her cherrywood desk with papers strewn all over it. I had my checkbook open, a gold pen in my hand, and didn't know who was supposed to get the money. It was very awkward.

"Oh," Sandra told me, "just leave it blank; I'll take care of it for you."

"She sure did, all right. She endorsed it right into her personal account. I was so dumb it took me months to figure out something was wrong. She was fined, which I understand is pretty standard, but it's still unclear whether she'll be barred permanently or just suspended for a while. What I'm really hoping is that the SEC (Securities Exchange Commission) will order her to pay my money back.

"The embarrassing thing is that I was so gullible. And not just me either. The Securities Exchange Commission says the fourth-most-common investment swindle is brokers depositing checks to their personal accounts. I sure didn't expect my inheritance to end up in some stranger's account."

"Allison, do you have something to add?" asked Joanne as she spied Allison's hand inching upwards. "Jump right in."

"It's just that this is amazing! A woman my mom knows at church told her last week that her stockbroker forged her name to a letter ordering $5,500 from the cash value in her life insurance policy. She didn't suspect a thing until she got a letter from her life insurance company confirming that they'd sent the money she requested. She called her broker immediately because he had sold her the policy. He told her he'd look into it, that it was probably a computer glitch.

"Well, as it turned out, it wasn't the computer at all. He'd ordered the money sent to his own office, forged her name to the check, and deposited it to his own account. She'd have never known if the insurance company had not followed their routine procedure of sending a letter to verify she'd received the check. Her broker was fined and barred from any association with any firm. And, because he had converted proceeds to his own use, he had to pay restitution."

"Ha!" Rose broke in. "How about what happened to my uncle? His broker got the insurance cash value, then forged an entire new life insurance application, got it issued, and was paid a commission on the new policy without my uncle even knowing. The new policy was sent to the broker's office for delivery, but the broker kept it and just forged his name on the delivery receipt. The broker made about $12,000 commission. Because the broker only forged my uncle's name — there was no conversation — he was fined and barred, but he didn't have to make restitution."

With that, Rhoda, who was sitting in the back of the room, started laughing. "Okay," she said through giggles, "I don't even remember where I heard this, but it just seemed so outrageous it was funny. There was a stockbroker who withdrew $25,000 from her client's securities account and then put it back about ninety days later! The broker made herself a short-term interest-free loan without her client's knowledge. It was discovered in a routine office audit, the kind they do to keep everyone on their toes."

Belinda, an older woman seated near the back of the room, spoke up next. "I think what happened to my college friend — the writer on the East Coast, whom I still correspond with — may take the cake. It began when she sent a $150,000 year-end royalty check to her broker to deposit in her account. Instead, he put most of it in his own account.

"He had an ingenious way of covering up so his customers wouldn't find out very quickly. He did it by substituting false monthly statements that showed all kinds of purchases and sales. Based on the statements, my friend thought she was making a nice profit. When the SEC started investigating, they discovered he was not even properly registered. His broker/dealer had been really sloppy about checking the status of his credentials!"

A gravelly voice broke into the conversation. Plainly dressed in black, and somewhat of a mystery, Ravenna joined the exchange.

"My dears, you've probably been thinking the brokers who did those things were drummed right out of the business, never to cheat another client. You're wrong.

"You see, my sister is a Certified Financial Planner. For nearly fifteen years she's been hearing stories like these, and she wanted to find out what happened to the brokers. Well, she learned there is no central agency that tracks how many complaints are filed in the various stock exchanges, much less how many are valid or how many brokers are drummed out of business.

"An article in one of the industry magazines reported that formal complaints to NASD (National Association of Securities Dealers) in the first half of 1995 were on their way to a record high of 5,000. Reasons for the increase were unclear, but it may be because there are more investors, and they are more willing to file formal complaints. Also, when markets are turbulent, more investors complain, so part of this may be fallout from 1994's market.

"An article in another magazine reported that more complaints are settled by arbitration than ever before. In 1991, plaintiffs won 54.6 percent of the NASD arbitration cases involving the public. In other words, more than half the time, investors are getting some satisfaction from their complaints.

"Then my sister wanted to learn how the brokers were punished. She tallied the cases reported in three of the 1995 quarterly issues of the NASD Regulatory & Compliance Alert. It reports only those cases in which penalties are assessed. There were 467 cases reported. Of those, 264 resulted in at least one person being 'barred from association with any NASD member in any capacity.' They were kicked out.

"In another nine cases at least one person was barred from having specific authority — it was like they were demoted — or they were required to apply again to be reaffiliated.

"In the other reported cases the broker and/or his firm was ordered to pay a fine, to make restitution to a client, to repay commissions, to requalify by test, or to sit out a short-term suspension.

"My sister also learned that NASD sanction guidelines ask that significant consideration be given to a history of offenses or to conduct that is egregious (excessive, extreme or outrageous). In other words, if there is a long history of offenses or the conduct is excessive, the punishment is likely to be more severe. Personally, I'd think it was excessive if it involved any of my money, even if it was the only time the broker did something like that!"

Ravenna stopped speaking. The silence lengthened.

Finally President Joanne remarked, "Well, I guess all this makes it imperative to investigate a broker or financial manager before we trust him or her with our money."

A Bit of Financial Wizardry

Your first line of defense is to make your investment checks payable to the appropriate entity. The second is to read your statements every single month. Find time now in your busy schedule or you may have to find even more time later trying to recover losses.

1. Always issue a check payable to either your

brokerage account or, in the case of mutual funds, limited partnerships and annuities, to the company from which you are purchasing. Make your check payable to your advisor only if you are expressly paying for his or her investment advice.
2. Always examine the endorsement on your check. Verify the account name and number to which it was deposited. If you have any doubts at all, start questioning!
3. Read every statement. Does it show unauthorized trades? Are your profits consistently smaller than the commissions? Does your statement show investments that don't match your objectives or your instructions? These are danger signs; get moving!
4. If you do not receive your statements, or if they begin arriving at a different time than they have been, ask questions.
5. If you need to double-check on your broker or insurance agent, talk to his or her supervisor, not them. Ask the supervisor to order a duplicate statement(s) and also verify that your address is correctly entered in their system.
6. If a problem is not resolved, write to the firm's Compliance Department. Your broker's own office

must provide you with the address. Just your asking for the Compliance Department's address is sure to get their attention!
7. You can also file a complaint with the appropriate agency(s). See the Appendix for information and addresses.

3

Ignorance is *Not* Bliss

Brandy was desperate when she called for an appointment with Marlene, a financial planner whose name she located in the Yellow Pages. Tearfully she said, "I should be in jail or dead because of the things I did. I need to get it back before she finds out!"

In her late thirties, unkempt, overweight, twisting one strand of mousy brown hair around and around her forefinger as she talked, Brandy told Marlene that she had worked for several years as a nurse, but since her move to a new state had let her license lapse. She was divorced from an abusive man and the single parent of Allison and Marti, ages twenty-one and seventeen.

Brandy explained, "My daughter Allison is legally blind from a medical accident. Four years ago she was awarded almost $650,000 in a malpractice settlement with her doctor. I planned to use part of the money for her education and to invest the rest so she'd have money to live on if she couldn't find work or needed something special."

Brandy slumped against the back of her chair, twisting a torn tissue in her hand as she struggled to continue her story.

"Marti is still in high school and looking for a college. She's outgoing, very talented, and plans to cram as many business courses as she can into her four years at university. She thought she'd get some of Allison's settlement for her education—oh, I just don't know how I'm going to face this!"

Brandy lost her struggle for composure as tears streamed down her face. Moments passed as she cried, blew her nose, and cleared her voice to resume.

"When the award was made, I talked to a financial planner, to a man at the bank, and to my attorney. Everyone said I should put the money in a trust to be professionally managed. They were talking about hundreds of dollars in fees. I felt like they were just

Ignorance is Not *Bliss*

trying to take it over. Where were they when I was fighting to get this money?

"Anyway, I decided it was our money; that we'd fought the system to get it, and I'd manage it myself. The first thing I did was to pay back the $42,000 my parents lent me for my divorce and some of the costs of the malpractice suit."

She said, "I didn't invest the rest because I didn't understand the market and I was afraid of losing it. So I just kept it in the bank where it was safe."

"I've been using it for living expenses of about $2500 a month, and we used it to pay for the move out here. We found a house in an older neighborhood with big trees and flowers. I've always wanted a nice home, not some dive of an apartment. I paid the whole price in one lump sum so I wouldn't have to worry about payments. You should have been the agent's face when I just wrote out a check for $220,000! It was great! Finally my girls have a nice place to bring their friends."

Marlene made notes as Brandy talked, trying to keep up with how much might be left from the original settlement. She sighed, fearing the worst, and readjusted her position in the chair.

"I'm nearly done," Brandy murmured. "The house needed furniture, so we got everything to match, no odds and ends this time! I got the girls nice music systems and—the most fun of all—is our two matching cherry-red loaded-with-everything cars. We have everything we ever dreamed about: a nice house, pretty furniture and jazzy cars.

Several moments passed, and Brandy's voice was subdued as she began again. "It wasn't until I looked at our account balance to pay the income taxes that I realized we had spent so much. I haven't been able to pay the IRS, and that worries me. We've had all this money, but now I'm back to worrying about paying bills. That's what brought me here.

"Allison doesn't know that her settlement is down to about $35,000! I just don't want to see her face when I tell her it is gone. I have to replace it: I have to find some way to get it back!! She'll hate me, and she'll be right to hate me! I deserve it! What can I do? Do you have an investment that can make it back? How can I tell them that neither one can go to college now? Oh, God, I wish I were dead! I blew it; I just blew it!"

Brandy was near collapse, her face contorted in tears, her anguish filling the room. The silence after her passionate outburst was startling.

Marlene waited for her to calm a bit before asking a series of questions. Then she told Brandy, "There is no fairy-godmother solution. What's done is done. The money can never be replaced. The best you can do is damage control.

"Here are my recommendations. First, you must tell the girls about your reduced situation so they can investigate loans and scholarships for their education. Others have gone to college without big settlements, so this is very possible. You can also apply to appropriate agencies for educational help for Allison.

"Next, get therapy for all of you, especially you, Brandy, as you need to be strong to handle all this. Don't put it off or think you don't need it; you're hating yourself right now and talking about dying. You made a mistake, that's all. Now it has to be dealt with.

"Brandy, find out what it will take to renew your professional nursing accreditation so you can support your family. Figure out your monthly expenses, then talk to the IRS about an income tax payment plan.

"You'll have to sell the cars or even the house if you can't afford their upkeep. You may even want to sell the house to replace part of Allison's settlement. That would give you back about $220,000, which you could split for college and investments. Only this time let a professional manage it!

"Lastly, look for a house to rent. You can still live in a nice area without owning it outright."

A Bit of Financial Wizardry

Unfortunately, Brandy's situation is not unusual. Lottery winners, heirs of mid-sized estates, divorcees who receive large settlements, and athletes who suddenly earn large salaries are all at risk as well.

What they all have in common is lack of experience managing money in such large amounts. They don't know the language, the players, the educational resources, or the warning signs. Often they are the only one in their circle of friends with this problem, so there is no one to talk with or, more painful still, they are marked as "rich" and asked for loans or handouts by family and friends.

4 Your Odds of Outwitting Your Broker Are About as Good as Winning the Lottery

Debbie was in her mid-twenties, tall and slender. Her straight brown hair, jeans and man's shirt blended with the no-nonsense world of trucking in which she and her husband were owner-operators. A serious woman, she thought she had a solution to keep honest the stockbrokers who called her. Even though Debbie's high school diploma did not prepare her for dealing with the jargon of the securities industry, she enjoyed the calls from the brokers because they made her feel important.

In a meeting with Selma, a young financial planner who was referred to her by a mutual friend, Debbie said, "I know there is a lot of money to be made with stocks, a lot more than what my husband makes by driving a truck. I want to make some good buys, and I know I can't afford to lose a lot. We already have accounts with two brokers, but I don't really trust either one of them after what I read in the papers about people being cheated. It's like I need a broker to make the trades, but I don't believe everything they say. They're probably not telling me all about the stocks they recommend.

"You're not the only broker who calls me, you know. I get calls every week from someone. They're probably working off some kind of a list. And I don't trust that either. How can they have time to call me, a stranger, if they're as successful as they want me to believe?"

Selma nodded sympathetically, her curly red-brown hair catching the afternoon sunlight as it streaked through Debbie's small office window and onto the worn brown textured carpet.

Debbie continued: "About three years ago I bought my first stocks. I remember they cost $5,300 because it seemed like such a huge check to write. The only reason I finally bought anything was that Adam—that's my broker's name—Adam, called about a bank stock he felt would do really well. That very morning I had read a newspaper article about how banks were turning around and that they would be a good place to invest some money. It was just meant to be."

Selma winced inwardly at Debbie's sincere belief that she had received a "special" message favoring her with exclusive information to buy bank stock.

"How did I find a second broker?" She responded in reply to a question from Selma, "Well, a few days after I bought the bank stock Boris called. He told me about a young company that manufactures a new type of battery. Batteries I understand, with our business that involves trucks! I bought one hundred shares and plan to get more. That's when I got The Idea.

"The reason I'm sharing this is that I want you to know I will double-check whatever you recommend to be sure it's something appropriate. I'm already doing that with the two brokers I have.

"Whenever one of my brokers calls with a buy recommendation I check with the other broker about its price and potential. I always say I'm asking for a "friend" who needs the information. It's been working fine. So I want you to know that I will check with either Boris or Adam about what it is you want me to buy."

Selma was silent for several long moments as she pondered how—or if—to tell Debbie the futility of her efforts. That her idea was like asking the fox about the coyote's intentions toward the henhouse.

"What Debbie did not realize," Selma said patiently, was that both of her brokers made recommendations with their own needs in mind. Both Adam and Boris have monthly sales quotas. Both receive commissions based on sales. If Debbie calls with a security she's excited about, the broker she's asking for verification will try to get her (or her "friend") to buy from him. If he doesn't have access to that particular security, he will discourage it or try to sell her something else.

Last month Adam, who sold her the bank stocks, called Debbie because he thought he could talk her into buying shares of a bank similar to the one she already owns. He was behind in his quota because he'd had the flu and had been off work a few days.

Last week Boris, who sold her the battery company, was under pressure to sell 5,000 shares of a small company as part of his broker-dealer's marketing campaign. He called her because it was a new company, and she seemed to like new companies.

Boris and Adam are each trying to convince

The Odds of Outwitting Your Broker Are About as Good as Winning the Lottery — 39 —

Debbie that he is looking out for her interests. Indeed, each must convince her if he is to meet his employer's monthly sales quota and survive in the business. And they've been trained to do it well.

In the last six months they probably attended training sessions with titles such as, "How to Sound Like a Million Dollars Over the Phone" or "The Right Stuff Prospecting Package."

Some investors try to double-check broker information by reading an expert's opinion in financial magazines and newsletters or by listening to radio and television programs. The information they glean is then used to grill their broker in the hopes of winnowing out "wrong" securities.

Gently, Selma tried to make Debbie understand that no investor has enough knowledge to trip up a well-trained stockbroker. Brokers spend as much time in sales classes as investors do in learning about specific investments. Selma told Debbie that she had a list of the twenty most common investor objections and a scripted answer to every one.

Selma said, "Debbie, you may say, 'I already have a broker.' Then I say, 'That's fine, but smart investors weigh all their options. Would it be all right if I call you with only my best ideas?' Are you going to object to hearing only my best ideas? Not usually.

"You say, 'I'm not interested in municipals.' I say, 'Oh, you have something you like better? What kind of securities have you had the most success in?'

"You say, 'I don't have any money.' I say, 'Very few smart investors have immediate cash available. While we're waiting for something to mature, I can search the market for you and we can do some planning.'

"You say, 'I don't know anything about money managers; can't my stockbroker do the same thing?' I say, 'Oh, someone with your investments should take advantage of custom account managing by a person who has a full-time staff doing nothing but research. I think I can arrange a place for you at our country club luncheon next week. You'll meet one of the best money managers in the country. It certainly doesn't hurt to check out all your options.'"

Another disadvantage for Debbie, Selma points out, is that she, like other investors, does not have the vocabulary to understand her broker's world. For instance, what's the difference between a Registered Representative, a Registered Investment Advisor and a

Certified Financial Planner? What is the difference between coupon rate, annual rate and effective rate? What's the difference between the underwriting broker, the offset broker, and the broker of record? More importantly, how does each affect Debbie's chances of success?

Selma, still patient and informative, offered Debbie some indisputable logic that destroyed her strategy of working with two brokers.

"Basically, Debbie, you're dealing with someone you do not trust. That's just not very smart! Would you go to a doctor you don't trust? To an attorney? Then why would you give your money to two brokers you already doubt?"

Selma concluded her lecture to Debbie by advising her to develop a strategy that would include a personal financial plan. A personal financial plan sets benchmark guidelines such as the overall balance between stocks and bonds; specific kinds of stocks and bonds; the dollar amount; risk tolerance; and overall targeted rate of return.

For instance, if Debbie's financial plan designates 10 percent for small company stocks and she has 15 percent, she knows she must sell something before she can buy a new small-sized company. Or, if her financial plan shows she needs only a 7 percent average return to reach her goals, she may not want to risk the volatility of small companies at all.

"Do you see what I mean, Debbie?" Selma asked. "Do you want me to help you build a personal investment plan?"

"Yes," Debbie said wisely, "then I'll have the right guidelines to weigh what my brokers are recommending."

A Bit of Financial Wizardry

First, develop a long-term strategy. Find a Registered Investment Advisor whom you can pay by the hour to develop a game plan. Especially when you're just starting out.

Then find one trustworthy person to help you buy appropriate securities. Look for:
1. A Certified Financial Planner and/or,
2. Someone referred by the International Association for Financial Planning in Denver, Colorado and/or,
3. A broker who's been in business at least five years,

The Odds of Outwitting Your Broker Are About as Good as Winning the Lottery – 43 –

4. Someone with a clean compliance record. You can check with your state authorities (try the Securities Division) about complaints,
5. Someone with appropriate registrations and licensing. While you're on the phone to your state regulators checking on any complaints, ask about this, too.

5

Romancing the Investment

"Mrs. Brown-Smythe, may I present Mr. Buckingham, the General Partner of Bridgeport Limited Partnerships. We have him to thank for this lovely reception."

Mrs. Brown-Smythe, a matronly woman in her early forties, extended her hand to Buckingham and said, "It's a pleasure to finally meet the man who is going to make me so much money! Please call me Evangeline; it seems silly to be formal when we're going to be partners."

"You are most kind, Madam. You may call me Bernard. I'm looking forward to a long and profitable relationship."

Mrs. Brown-Smythe and Buckingham were standing to one side of a carpeted ballroom in a luxury hotel. She was dressed in a tailored hot-pink suit accessorized with a multi-colored scarf held in place at her shoulder by a large diamond pin. Her red hair was flawlessly fashioned in a French twist that effectively displayed the dangling diamond earrings that matched her pin. Buckingham was wearing a classic-cut blue suit, burgundy paisley tie, and stiff white shirt whose French cuffs were fastened with diamond cufflinks. His balding head, with its halo of auburn hair, caught the lights as he nodded to the guests. Mrs. Brown-Smythe was dressed to exhibit her ability to invest; he was decked out to instill confidence in his success and trustworthiness.

Around the two swirled about a hundred guests, many of whom were balancing drinks and hors d'oeuvres as they made their way to the straight-backed chairs arranged in rows at one end of the ballroom. Mrs. Brown-Smythe had attended such receptions before. She knew that in a few minutes Buckingham would address the gathering, discussing the limited partnership for which he was general partner. Usually that involved presenting a business plan and projections sufficiently alluring to induce most of the guests present to write a check payable, of course, to his partnership.

Mrs. Brown-Smythe said to Buckingham, "Bernard, before you have to go away and meet your other investors, tell me about this restaurant. I hear you've got some of Disney's old people involved."

"Well, yes, we do. Some animators who used to be with that studio and wanted to do something different." Skillfully he sidestepped the direct connection to the world-famous studio inferred by her question.

"I'm very excited about our concept," he said. "We think a restaurant catering to families will be very successful, especially with our concept of automated entertainment. Our animators have created a singing and playing hillbilly band of bears. New programs will be developed regularly so families can come back again and again. Animation is going to be big in the entertainment field, and we're one of the first to jump in. The idea is that parents can turn their kids loose to play in a safe environment while they wait for their meals. Have a casual evening out. The first restaurant is under construction as we speak, and we intend to build the second right here in this city. We'll be checking sites in the next couple days to get an idea of what's available.

In the next ten years we project at least six total restaurants in several states."

"Excuse me, Bernard," interrupted a short pot-bellied man who had approached. "I just wanted you to meet my client, Mr. Shaw, who invested his pension rollover with you. He wanted to know the man who's going to turn his $80,000 into $150,000."

Seamlessly Buckingham greeted Mr. Shaw, shook his hand, and sent him on his way. Meeting investors was something he had done many times.

The reception was a success, with more than 50 percent of the guests investing. Mrs. Brown-Smythe's check was for $110,000. The idea of being in on a deal involving animation, working with people from the studio most famous for that very thing, and helping young families while making nice profits was impossible for her to resist.

Unanticipated by the cheery group is a future in which within two years the partnership would have cash flow problems; in four years it would be in bankruptcy proceedings; and in eight years nonexistent. The stiff competition among restaurants, a poor location, and a regional economy turned sour combined to cause the collapse.

Two thousand miles away, in a far more casual setting, an investor is getting bad news of another sort.

"What do you mean the stallion is dead?! I have $10,000 in that horse; he can't have died! Gail's jaw was clenched and she beat the air with her fists. In her late twenties and overweight, every bulge was profiled by her jeans and T-shirt. Her long blonde braid slapped against her hips as she paced.

"I want my $10,000 back. Forget the profit I was supposed to make; just get me back my original investment!"

"I wish I could, Gail, I wish I could." The speaker was Amandee, Gail's financial planner, and the person who recommended the limited partnership. "The money has been spent. Remember, a partnership is an operating business with ongoing business expenses. Caring for a stallion is expensive. There's his groom, the veterinarian, his trainer, his feed, even the equipment. Everyone who bought a share of him expected to make a profit on his stud fees. After all, pure Egyptian Arabians are rare in this country, and he was in demand."

Gail stopped pacing to glare at Amandee. "I've always wanted a horse. For as long as I can remember I wanted a horse. This was a way to own one, a really nice one. I owned part of a beautiful animal. Now you tell me he's dead!! I should have bought my own, even if it wasn't as nice, and boarded it until I had a place to keep it. At least I'd have something now."

"Gail," Amandee gently interrupted. "No one knows why he died. The vet's report isn't back yet. You could have lost a horse in your own care. They're living animals, and they can get sick. That was one of the risks."

"I don't care!! It was all so wonderful, being part of the horse world, owning such a rare kind of horse, a five-million-dollar horse!"

"Are you saying you would not have invested if it had been a different horse? That it was the glamour of that particular bloodline, and all that goes with it, that attracted you?"

"Well, why else would I have put up my money?"

A Bit of Financial Wizardry

In the 1980s, many small investors were presented with opportunities to invest in ways previously available only to the very wealthy. Thousands put dollars into limited partnerships that promised both tax advantages and profit. Then, in 1986, tax law changes were enacted by Congress and, for the first time, there was no grandfathering of existing business contracts. That's a risk whenever you invest: the tax laws could be changed.

Limited partnerships began collapsing by the hundreds. Some were poorly planned in the first place and would have collapsed anyway. Others, which should have succeeded, were dealt a death blow by tax laws that eliminated their tax advantage and drove potential investors away. Investors already committed could not get their money out.

The sizzle can get your attention, but if there isn't a good steak beneath it, walk away. Determining that will take some serious number-crunching by both you and your tax advisor.

6 Blowing Smoke in Your Advisor's Face is Dangerous to Your Wealth

Don and Rusty were both disabled, he from arthritis and she from both arthritis and a heart condition. Each of them used a cane to help them walk, and they looked ten years older than their mid-sixties. Theirs was a long traditional marriage, still full of love for each other.

Rusty stood ramrod straight and had difficulty bending because of her arthritic spine. Her graying hair was neatly arranged around well-balanced features. She was sweet-voiced, proper in her manner, and deferred to Don in family decisions. Her role was raising their five children.

Don slouched around a prominent belly and had

trouble with his knees. His unruly white hair surrounded a beaming face, from which came forth a gruff voice. His high school education served him well as manager of a service station.

"We want to move our trust account to you, Carol," Don said while Rusty nodded agreement.

Carol was a successful financial planner. "We heard you on the radio talk show and decided you're the person for us. Five years ago we inherited $400,000 from Rusty's folks. At first, we left all of it with the manager who'd been taking care of it for our folks, but we didn't like owing so much for taxes when we weren't taking income from it. Everyone acted like they had more say over it than we did, so we took our part and moved it up here to a new manager about eighteen months ago. The problem is, we still don't understand our reports. When we heard your easy-to-understand radio talk, we knew we wanted to work with you!"

Carol took her time getting to know Don and Rusty while she developed a profile of risk tolerance and goals. She explained each step of the transfer process, documents they would receive, and what their fees would be. She also helped them locate an attorney to act as trustee. All four of them met to finalize the investment strategy before trades were begun.

All went well with the new relationship for two years. The market went up. The portfolio grew. Don and Rusty received monthly income. Their attorney received brokerage reports on time. Then the couple began withdrawing larger and larger amounts from the trust.

"Carol," they explained, "our oldest son is out of work and needs a little help."

"Carol, we just found out we can get motorized wheelchairs at a real good price."

"Carol, we need to get away for a few days."

"Carol, our daughter doesn't have the money to come for the holidays."

"Carol, we want to get a second medical opinion and our insurance won't pay for it."

"Carol, it's time to pay the taxes on the little rental house we're letting our youngest son live in."

Carol found herself concerned and advised the couple, "You are withdrawing from your trust faster than it earns. You have to leave some profit in so it can grow; if you keep going into principal the trust will self-destruct."

Both Carol and the couple's attorney urged them to "Please, stay within budget. You have to let your kids know that you can't keep bailing them out. Your trust is not that large, and you are depleting it! You'll be living on just your Social Security if you aren't more careful."

Each time they were warned, Don agreed with smiling eyes and bobbing head. They would cut back "next month," or when he paid a "certain bill." Rusty didn't challenge his decisions.

Another year passed, and of the original $400,000, only $120,000 was left, barely enough to cover the couple's needs for two years, much less gifts to their children. Carol was finding it more and more difficult to trade; the portfolio was at critical mass. She was distressed that there was not enough time to let new purchases age, or for recovery from downward fluctuation because of the constant withdrawals.

Then, from a remark made in passing by Don, Carol discovered he had been using part of the trust distributions to dabble in mutual funds.

"Carol," Don finally said when he realized he had slipped, "our financial-advice newsletter thinks it will do real well, so I bought some shares. It's supposed to balance a couple of the others we already bought. I'd like to know more about it and I'd like you to check on it for me. I might as well tell you I also bought some

Chinese gold coins for Rusty. They're something she can wear while they're getting more valuable. The newsletter said there are only a few minted each year."

When Carol reminded Don that he promised to stay within budget, he replied, "You'll just have to make the trust keep growing for us!"

Carol resigned from the account before the end of the week. The relationship had become intolerable for her when she realized that Don would not change his unrealistic spending habits. For him to hide mutual fund investments which had been made from the distributions he received was the last straw.

Don did not understand that the money he used for mutual funds and coins depleted the trust. If he wanted to have a "play account," he should have taken it from their budgeted cash flow, not asked for phony special distributions.

Worse yet, he did not realize the mutual fund so highly touted in his newsletter was not suitable for them; it was volatile and recommended only for long-term growth portfolios. He refused to understand that investment-quality gold coins were never worn next to human skin because the acid destroys them. He failed to appreciate that Carol could not magically "make it grow." He also failed to comprehend, even with all the graphs she furnished and the meetings she arranged, that the trust would go bankrupt at Don and Rusty's current level of withdrawals despite its earnings.

Rusty died two years later while undergoing surgery on her hip. Don inherited her trust. In a few months he remarried.

In less than three years his second wife went through all his assets: the trust, the mutual funds, the coins, the cash account, and two rental houses. She divorced him. Don was living on Social Security when he died.

His children searched vainly for the inheritance he had promised. The only thing left was his residence, which was in need of repairs.

A Bit of Financial Wizardry

Deceiving your financial advisor — or your attorney — is not a wise thing to do. It can be fatal to your family's financial health!

For any planning to be accurate and for any portfolio to perform, all pertinent information must be disclosed.

Never, ever lie!

7 How to Lose Your Shirt with "Shortcut" Reports

The general inclination of people to avoid reading financial reports extends to brokerage statements as well, and has resulted in a rather common scheme to defraud investors of millions of dollars. Let's discover what happened to Paul because of his failure to peruse important financial information about his investments. Paul was a mid-level manager in the electronics industry. Quiet, a man who looked more like a schoolboy than a mature thirty-year-old, he accepted a challenging position in a city halfway across the country. Soon he was interviewing Jeff, a broker, about transferring his $350,000 brokerage account.

"I'm trying to get as much done this week as

– 59 –

possible because I start my new job on Monday. I found an apartment I really like. I go from here to the bank to get an account set up. And I want to move my stock account. Will you tell me a little about yourself, your clients, and how long you've been a broker?"

Jeff gave Paul the information he wanted and the pair hit it off right away, perhaps because of a shared love of golf.

Paul was exuberant about Jeff's intuitive understanding of what he wanted to accomplish with his investments. "Wow. This is wonderful! It's as if you read my mind. You understand I want to retire early, but do not want to take a lot of risk to get there. I am relieved that I won't have to be involved day to day with this account while I am settling in and starting my new job. This job is a wonderful chance for me: I need to hit the ground running."

"Jeff smiled and said, "I have developed a service for my busier clients. I'll send you a summarized monthly report that is easier to understand and quicker to read than the one my company is required to send. You'll get them both, but if your schedule is really as tough as you think it may be, you could read mine and come back to the other one when you have more time."

How to Lose Your Shirt with "Shortcut" Reports – 61 –

All went well for Paul for several months. He put in long hours at his office; Jeff called regularly just to chat, and the reports Paul read showed his portfolio's value steadily increasing. Then, Paul found a wonderful house with hardwood floors and a three-mountain view.

The mortgage lender required a copy of the "real" brokerage statement, so, for the first time since he opened his account with Jeff, Paul read a monthly company report — not the summary Jeff had been sending.

"Jeff, what is going on?! I'm looking at my brokerage statement, and it does not agree with the one you've been sending! This one shows me with small company stocks, not the solid blue chips your report shows. Besides, there must be a mistake in the value! The brokerage statement places my value at nearly $75,000 less than what I put in!"

"Paul, the mistake must be in the computers; you know how that is. Garbage in, garbage out. Let me check on it for you, and I'll call you back. Takes only a couple days."

Instead, Paul raced to the brokerage firm to see Jeff's manager.

Paul discovered during the ensuing investigation

that Jeff had made unauthorized trades in his account. Jeff covered his transactions up by using his own address to get the trade confirms so Paul would never see them. Jeff also ordered money from Paul's account paid to himself and falsified the value on his own "special" reports to cover it up.

Paul was not the only one cheated; there were at least nine others, and total losses were well over $640,000. Jeff was fined $100,000 and permanently barred from associating with any NASD firm in any capacity. He was also ordered to make restitution.

A Bit of Financial Wizardry

Brokerages are required by SEC regulation to provide investors with monthly statements for their own protection. The statements detail all the activity for the month. However, there is no protection if they lie unopened and unread in a drawer.

If a report has anything to do with your money, read it! This applies to your securities, insurance policies, home mortgage contract, warranties, loan documents, service contracts, and even your will!

Read your documents with a notebook in one hand

How to Lose Your Shirt with "Shortcut" Reports

and a pen for taking notes in the other. If you have doubts — or don't understand — start asking questions. Persist until you get understandable, dependable answers no matter how many times you have to ask.

When you are asking questions, especially in the buying stage, act as dumb as you can possibly be. You are going to be as thick as a brick. Use open-ended questions such as, "Can you explain that in a different way?" or, "I still don't quite understand how this works," or, "Is there another way to do this?"

Questions like these work like magic to provide information you wouldn't have even thought to ask about. Don't get caught by one of the Jeffs of the world. Protect yourself by keeping abreast of what your investments are doing.

8

Trusting Your Hunch

"I just have this feeling that something is not right. There's nothing specific, but it has been nagging at me."

Naomi sat on the edge of a wingback chair across from Alice, a reputable financial planner. Naomi's medium-brown hair was combed straight down from a center part and fell just below her ears. She was a small woman, barely a hundred pounds, with large, thick glasses pushed firmly against the bridge of her nose. Her hazel eyes, magnified by her glasses, dominated her face. Her short, quick movements and angular facial planes combined to remind Alice of an alert mouse.

Speaking with precision, she said, "My husband died eight months ago. I'm pretty well set as far as money goes. Our house was paid off with his mortgage insurance, and my investments total over one million, one hundred ten thousand. Our broker said he would take care of the investments, and that is what I'm feeling concerned about."

Naomi blinked and took a deep breath. Then she patted the paper-filled brown manila envelope lying on the desk near her elbow. It contained a monthly statement from her broker. She continued, "My husband and I have been with this broker for years. Even though my husband actually talked with him, we jointly made all the decisions affecting our investments. I was involved every step of the way. I know exactly what we — I — own and why it was chosen.

However, our — my — broker is treating me like an intruder. The last time we talked he said for me to leave the investments to him because he knew what my husband would have wanted. He had the audacity to suggest that I go bake cookies and stop worrying myself about this. The reason I came to you is that I need an outside opinion. My broker is still recommending limited partnerships, but we bought them before to shelter my husband's income. Now I think I need securities for growth and income. And I need a way to make my broker listen to me."

Alice made a list of the information she needed. In a few days Naomi delivered her tax returns, brokerage statements, and prospectuses, a stack of paper more than twenty inches high!

"I've discovered a bit of a problem," she said to Alice. "I don't have all the things you need, and I don't get reports about the limited partnerships from the brokerage company. They're not listed anywhere on my statement; it's as if they dropped out of sight. I have no idea what their current status is, and I'm wondering if even my broker knows!"

After discussion, the two women agreed that Naomi would make phone calls to the general partners to get the needed information. Alice made a list of the partnerships and the questions. Ten days later Naomi called her back.

"Alice, I'm getting good response from my calls, and I'm learning a lot! Several of the service reps were startled at the technical accuracy of my questions. Thanks to you! I made a chart with the partnership names across the top and the questions down one side. It's hanging over my washing machine so I can see it every day. Most of the blanks have been filled in. The few remaining partnerships should call by the end of next week."

Alice set about determining how, with minimum changes, Naomi's portfolio could be turned into an income-producing one that could also stay ahead of inflation and taxes.

At their next meeting Alice said, "Naomi, your instinct was correct: your portfolio needs a change of focus. Presently, it provides $40,000 in tax shelter, but only $20,000 income. In other words, it is badly out of balance, absent your husband's salary."

"But what does that mean?"

"It means that you should not buy any more tax-sheltered investments. Concentrate instead on growth and income. Also, you'll need to keep your chart because it tells year by year what the general partners project for future write-off. Your CPA will want that information. As you know, it's next to impossible to sell a limited partnership for anything near what you paid for it. So this is the next best thing. You'll use the write-off until it's used up or the partnerships terminate.

"I identified which securities you should sell," Alice said, "and also the current interest rates for bonds, CDs and treasuries with which to replace them. After you reposition, you should have $60,000 income, of which $40,000 will be sheltered.

Naomi's confident remark as she left Alice was, "It was worth your $2,000 fee. Now I've got the facts to deal with my broker. If he doesn't listen to me, I'll simply find someone else. Bake cookies indeed!"

Several months later Alice heard from Naomi. She learned that Naomi was still with her broker, but that he's not second-guessing her anymore. It turned out that she knew more about the limited partnerships than he did, so he had to acknowledge her skill!

A Bit of Financial Wizardry

There are two reasons for sharing Naomi's story here. The first is that she trusted her hunch. Many times the first indication of problems is that "something does not feel right." If Naomi had ignored the instinct which warned her against following her broker's recommendations, the consequences could have been disastrous.

The second reason is that women investors are treated differently from men. In June 1993, *Money Magazine* reported on a test it did in which they sent two groups of "investors" (fifty men and women) to several different brokerages. One group was younger and had $25,000 to invest; the second, older, group had $50,000 to invest. They each had identical salaries, investment experience, portfolios and goals.

Money reported the test revealed that women are treated differently — usually less well — by brokers than they treat men. The brokers tell men about a wider range of investments and explain them better. And they try harder to sign up men as customers. The report did note that women were treated *more courteously.*

Good advice is for you to trust your hunches; act on your hunches; and remember that not all brokers who market to women think women are competent.

9 Deceptions and Distortions: Con Games People Play

People are fascinated with con artists because they seem to demonstrate imagination and craftiness, notwithstanding a predatory bent of mind. It is worthwhile knowing about some of the more common "con games" that are played out on innocents if for no other reason than to be able to recognize and avoid them.

I'll start by addressing the factors I believe make a con—confidence—game as distinguished from misrepresentation. A confidence game is a calculated *deception* involving trickery, falsification and gimmicks. Other names for con games are bunco games, shell games, boiler room tactics, etc. On the other hand, misrepresentation is a calculated *distortion,* a falsification. Something is being sold, but its value or the opportunity it represents is distorted.

Both of these methods to dishonestly relieve people of their money result in severe financial losses to the client, and many can cause emotional distress. In one case an emotional response took the life of a man who lost a lot of money when his broker invested him too aggressively in the stock market.

Following are some actual cases of con games and misrepresentation:

The first involves a licensed stockbroker of a major national firm. In 1992, she and her firm were charged in a class-action suit alleging that she sold unsuitable investments to over six hundred clients. The charges were that she "churned" accounts and that at least one of the investments was a municipal (bond) trust which was not appropriate for her clients because none of them were in high enough tax brackets to benefit. A key contention of the investigators was that the investors were very unsophisticated people and she took advantage of their naiveté by opening margin accounts. Margin accounts can be borrowed against, and are for experienced investors. She convinced her investors to "borrow" against hoped-for profits in order

Deceptions and Distortion
Con Games People Play

to buy more securities. The attorney for the plaintiffs said his clients lost $10,000 to $30,000 each.

In another case, in 1988, a financial planning firm in the Midwest promoted nonexistent "government-backed bonds" to about a hundred investors as a means of funding their children's education. The investors lost over three million dollars, and the firm's recoverable assets were only about $400!

In 1988 in the South, a former church pastor offered "Christian Financial Planning" to churches and their congregations. He promised 15 percent to 18 percent return on "consumer savings certificates." There were no such securities, and the money was never invested. The pastor pocketed it. About sixteen investors lost a total of $226,000.

One of the fanciest schemes was perpetrated in Chicago by a financial planner who targeted investors nearing retirement age. He put together a complex web of trusts and 350 real-estate limited partnerships. More than 6,000 people lost $45 million!! The money was never invested; it went to three homes for the planner, along with a 26-foot boat, aircraft, an aircraft hangar, and motor vehicles.

Then there was the man on the East Coast who

was sentenced to 222 years in prison for a phony investment pool scheme in which forty investors in eight states, including his wife's grandmother, lost a total of $1.3 million.

On the West Coast there was a thirty-year-old financial planner with a successful practice who strayed from the straight and narrow. Instead of investing in stocks and bonds, he put clients' money into an Ohio firm that tried to market floating sunglasses. To perpetrate the scheme and keep it going, he paid off earlier investors with money from later investors in a fraud known as a Ponzi scheme. The person worst hit was a widow whose $300,000 insurance proceeds disappeared.

There was the case of the rabbit swindle in which a slickster in the Southwest sold limited partnerships for a business in which genetically superior rabbits were to be bred for their pelts. He promised that the pelts would be sold to high-priced department stores and the meat to South Korean mercenaries guarding Saudi Arabian oil fields. Seventy people put up $1.2 million. They recovered $50,000.

For the fraud with the most chutzpah, the Ponzi scheme from San Diego took the cake. A mild-

Deceptions and Distortion
Con Games People Play

mannered, quiet-spoken man with thick glasses and a three-piece suit opened a brokerage firm and started selling "international currency transactions" which he asserted would generate 40 percent gains. This man sold to the mayor, prominent business and social leaders, politicians, doctors, lawyers, judges, accountants, stockbrokers, developers and military officers. One investor was so taken by the idea that he put in $42 million. The total take on the scheme? $200 million. Investors' money went to pay prior investors to keep the ball rolling and into the pockets of the schemer. Exorbitant returns were deliberately paid to some investors in order to entice more suckers.

Widows were swindled in Utah by a moonlighting church organist who sold them phony bonds. He spotted them while playing at their husbands' funerals. One widow checked with her bishop and got a favorable report, so she thought it was okay. That's common in swindling schemes: they're sold by word of mouth on the recommendation of a friend or a relative.

Between 1986 and 1988, investors lost more than $396 million because of fraud and abuse in the financial planning stock brokerage industry. In almost all cases, the schemes depended on the confidence the investor had in his advisor. Frauds of the nature I've described happen partly because of the nature of the investment industry itself. The average financial planning firm is small, composed of three to four people, so it's not unusual for an investor to work with a small office. That makes it easy for a con artist to set up a small operation and have it look credible. Everyone remembers the large firms because of name familiarity, but they are only a small piece of the pie.

Also, there are planners new to the industry who may have less actual investment experience than their clients. In many cases, the only difference between broker and client is that the broker has passed a test on laws governing the offering of investments to the general public. A new planner's or broker's mistakes are usually made out of ignorance, not malice.

However, advisors who have had a bankruptcy, or previous run-ins with state securities agencies, or have outstanding court judgments or felony convictions are a different breed of cat. As an example — and a pat on the back for the state agency that refused to approve his license transfer — a broker who signed a settlement agreement to repay a woman for taking $35,000 in IRA funds admitted that he was a compulsive gambler. When he applied to transfer to a new broker/dealer, the state refused to approve it, effectively pushing him out of the business. But what if he had been successful? He would have continued to handle other people's money, putting it at risk against his compulsion.

A Bit of Financial Wizardry

There are several warning signs of which you should be aware. These may not eliminate all the fraudulent schemes, but they, along with your common sense, should get the most. Just remember: When in Doubt, Don't!

1. Don't buy based on an unrealistically high yield. If it sounds too good to be true, it probably is.
2. Deal with an established business and/or with a broker who has been in business at least five years. Check both the broker's and the firm's compliance record with your state securities division.
3. Don't buy based on a guarantee without knowing what it is that's guaranteed.
4. Don't invest in anything that cannot be explained to your satisfaction in only a few words. Complicated deals, discretionary deals, or deals solicited over the

phone are more often higher risk and must be analyzed very carefully. Get your attorney or tax preparer involved.
5. Don't buy just because a friend or relative does. Even if it's a great deal, it still may not be appropriate for your risk tolerance or goals.
6. Don't put all your eggs in one basket. The purpose of diversification is to protect against risk. Use it.
7. Start investigating immediately if you suspect something is wrong, even if it's after you've invested. If your suspicions are not calmed, demand your money back. A threat to go to state regulators and/or the FBI can often be effective.
8. Know that you're your own first line of defense. Regulators do the best they can, but you have to look out for you.

10 Can I Trust You With My Money? Or, Is That Rock For Real?

Have you seen the ad of the Rock of Gibraltar on TV; it's meant to signify the stability, steadfastness and sincerity of the company for which it stands: Prudential. Millions of people have been reassured by The Rock, including Louise, a feisty and independent eighty-year-old widow.

Louise lived on her husband's Social Security benefits, interest from CDs, and an investment account. She was in good health, still did her own housework, and enjoyed puttering in her garden. She visited monthly with her son and his family, who lived forty minutes away.

Louise's stockbroker called her one spring

morning in 1984 just as she was finishing a strong cup of raspberry tea. "Louise, I can get you in on an investment that will give you a comparatively safe, predictable and steady source of income. You've been reading about how high gas prices have risen, haven't you? Well, you should get your share of the profit; it shouldn't go to just the big guys. The way this deal is put together the return will be between 15 and 20 percent. The wonderful thing is that every property is approved by Prudential Insurance itself. It's going fast, so you can't dawdle over your decision."

Louise was so pleased about a high *and* safe return she immediately invested more than $80,000 as fast as she could get the money out of her bank.

The investment was not safe and predictable. She lost it all.

Gene, who lived two thousand miles from Louise, received a call from his broker the same week Louise invested her money. A retired engineer living in a manufactured home on five acres along a tree-shaded creek, he too augmented his Social Security income from investments.

"I called about a real estate opportunity," his broker told him. "Prudential Life Insurance is the largest investor in their own program....They are putting their money where their mouth is." Gene was so impressed with Prudential's rock-solid reputation that he laid out $15,000. He lost more than three-quarters of it.

More than 320,000 Prudential-Bache (as the company was known pre-1991) customers invested millions and millions of dollars in real estate limited partnerships. In the sparsely populated state of Oregon alone more than $25 million was generated by phone calls from brokers who carefully followed the telephone scripts developed by their managers.

However, the deals were flawed from the beginning and, to make it worse, unexpected tax law revisions passed by Congress in 1986 made it much worse. In December 1993, the *Wall Street Journal* announced that Prudential Securities Inc. had agreed to pay at least $371 million to settle claims from investors who claimed losses from just over half to the entire amount invested.

The Securities Exchange Commission (SEC) investigation uncovered documents revealing that Prudential Insurance had deliberately used its "solid as a rock" image in the marketing of not-so-solid limited partnerships, including:

- allowing its insurance agents to sell the partnerships without being licensed to do so;
- instructing Prudential-Bache brokers in 1986 to tell its customers, "Remember: The general partner is Prudential — solid as a rock...Prudential Insurance is the largest private owner of real estate in the world. Without question, the strongest general partner in existence...Get a Piece of the Rock."
- Informing investors in a 1984 promotional tape for energy partnerships that every partnership property "is approved by Prudential Insurance itself."

Loretta, a widowed Florida retiree, spoke for many of the investors when she said, "The only reason I bought the partnerships was because I owned Prudential life insurance and believed in the company's integrity."

In this example, according to the investigators, two large companies, Prudential Life Insurance and Pru-Bache, capitalized on their advertising promotions and sterling business reputations. Other investment firms have also been fined for either their own infractions or for those of their brokers, as evidenced by newspaper releases regarding Shearson, Merrill Lynch, Dean Witter, Salomon Brothers and others. Unfortunately, their investors believe in each firm's reputation as

Can I Trust You With My Money?
Or, Is That Rock for Real?

presented by a skillful ad campaign.

Sadly, in Florence's case, she became a victim of institutional apathy. Florence was in her early fifties and her second marriage. Her trust was established by her parents to provide income for her during her lifetime. Whatever was left at her death was to pass to her three daughters.

It was Florence's intention that her daughters inherit at least as much as she did. She was an astute investor, followed the market, analyzed her bank statements, and consulted regularly with her trust officer. She was unhappy about long-standing problems with her bank's administration and investment services and complained to her trust officer, a man who recently transferred from Texas.

Her four-million-dollar trust account had been trusteed by a major regional bank for six years. The bank, as trustee, made investments, paid distributions to her under the terms of the trust, prepared and filed the trust's tax returns, dealt with legal matters that arose and, since Florence was co-trustee, received instructions from her. Central to her trustee's duties was that the trust be administered in accordance with tax regulations, trust laws, and the trust document itself. Florence paid a fee for the trustee to do these things.

In an interview with her new trust officer, Florence said, "Del, I appreciate that you have just been transferred to this bank and are trying to resolve my complaints about an account with which you are not familiar. Thank you for working so hard on this. However, I am more concerned than ever about the bank's capability. I thought my file would have the information needed to resolve this, but it doesn't. Instead, we have uncovered additional problems. That really dismays me."

"Florence," Del replied in his soft southern drawl, "I want to resolve this so everyone is happy. I'll do everything I can to help you."

Unmollified, Florence said, "The bank has lost three years of my trust's income tax returns; there are no records of the reduced-fee agreement my prior trustees and I negotiated five years ago, and there are no records of my discussions with my trust officer's assistant about the bank's current proposed huge — 24 percent! — increase in the trust fees. In addition, there are no records of my repeated calls over the last four years about the quarterly income distributions being too high. And just last quarter this bank sent me $250,000 as income when it is supposed to be about $30,000! That is outrageous.

Her disappointment mirrored in her face, Florence said, "Del, mistakes just seem to happen over and over. My feeling is that the bank simply does not have a proper management system in place. Furthermore, I just found out that the bank provides trust services about which I was never told. And there is a contract the bank and I should have signed when I moved the trust here. No wonder it's become impossible to sort through the current problems — there is not even a common starting point!"

Del was making notes as fast as he could and nodded to acknowledge his full attention.

"Even the bank's investment officer goofed," Florence said. "Investments have not been repositioned as we agreed. My Registered Investment Advisor — I hired an outside consultant — calculated that the trust will go bankrupt — there won't be anything for my daughters unless its rate of return is higher and/or the trustee fees are lower. I never dreamed that bankruptcy could be a real threat for a four-million-dollar account!

"Speaking of trustee fees," she continued, "I've been checking around. Did you know that your bank charges 50 to 100 percent more for trust services than its major competitors?"

Florence left Del's office with his promise that he would get to the "bottom of things" ringing in her ears.

He researched available records and talked with involved bank personnel. Reluctantly he acknowledged to himself that there were not enough notes in the bank's files to clearly establish the history of Florence's trust account. It was obvious to him that there were serious problems with the administration and investment of her trust. However, it was Florence's word against the bank's as to what the original expectations were.

There were several more meetings at which the bank's officers maintained, "We thought we were doing what you wanted; it's just a miscommunication." Never was there any acknowledgement that the bank's own lack of internal management systems may have created some of the problems, breach of fiduciary trust, and loss of earnings for Florence.

Florence was angry, but she was also savvy. And the savvy thing was to move the account, not to pay an attorney to fight with the bank. She knew that she would have to prove that her losses were the result of something considerably more than a miscommunication or a conflict between bank policy and her assumptions. She began the long process of interviewing new trustees and transferring the trust.

A Bit of Financial Wizardry

Large institutions have large marketing budgets to position themselves as problem-solver for every viewer or listener. They are not.

You will not be dealing with people who reflect the integrity implied by "The Rock" and other symbols of investment safety and responsibility. You will be dealing with flesh-and-blood people who make mistakes, who get transferred, who retire. Some of the people will be wonderful at what they do; some will not. You will like some of the people; some you won't trust.

You must perform due diligence even, or especially, when dealing with large institutions which have their own protective internal policies. You must determine if the policies of the institution, including its investment style, are appropriate for your situation.

Always ask questions, the more detailed the better.
Always get understandings in writing.
Keep your own log of conversations with persons

advising about or managing your securities, especially if it is an institution. That way you'll have a record in case the person to whom you talked retires or moves away.

11
Unsuitable, Inappropriate and Unfit

"Why not buy her some shares of that new start-up company? She needs growth, and it looks like everything else she owns is pretty conservative."

Everett had accompanied his recently widowed mother to her financial planner's office for her semi-annual review. A few years out of college, he took seriously his self-appointed task of watching out for her. He was only slightly more knowledgeable about the stock market than she was and was determined to learn as much as he could as fast as he could. He was aided by a natural ability to ask the right questions.

Ingrid, his mother, was a first-generation citizen, having fallen in love with an American GI stationed in her country. During their marriage he handled all financial affairs, including the writing of checks. She raised their son, tended a beautiful flower garden, and managed the household with an allowance he provided. She, too, was learning how to manage her affairs.

"The stock in a start-up company is not appropriate, Everett," said Polly, Ingrid's financial planner. Polly, sitting at a conference table across from Everett and his mother, was in her late fifties, slender with short curly graying hair. She had spent considerable time in the past fourteen months answering questions and recommending reading materials to Ingrid and her son. Now she focused her attention on Everett, understanding the protective feeling he had for his mother. "Everett, there are certain guidelines the SEC imposes independent of what clients say they want to do. There are several reasons I have not recommended, and will not, the type of stock you're asking about.

"The first is that your mother has never invested before; she has no experience in the stock market, especially in the volatility of new companies. Therefore she can't make an informed decision about the level of risk this would entail.

"Second, she has no way to replace this money

Unsuitable, Inappropriate and Unfit

should it be lost.

"Third, she needs an income on which to live; your father's Social Security is not enough. Moneys invested in interest- or dividend-bearing securities will cover the shortfall between Social Security and her needs. However, a start-up company does not pay dividends.

"Fourth, we spent considerable time designing a comprehensive financial plan before investments were made. Her plan has been in effect less than a year. It is too soon to make changes unless there is a major change in goals."

Polly had been looking directly at Everett as she delivered her lecture and was relieved that he seemed to agree with the investment strategy.

Polly continued, "On the other hand, a start-up company could be appropriate for your own investments for all the reasons it is not right for your mother. When you're ready to invest, let's look for one."

Polly was giving her clients wise advice. She knew the situation and her primary client's risk tolerance. Although there are many brokers who are conscientious, there are too many who do not take the time to understand the client's situation or make the erroneous assumption that the client knows more about investing than she actually does.

Inappropriate recommendations are not confined to brokers or financial planners; often bank trustees fail to perform properly on behalf of their clients, as the following story indicates:

Shirley was thirty-five years old and worked full time. She was the widowed parent of two children. Her husband's will had named their bank as trustee for his $500,000 life insurance proceeds. In the six months since his death, Shirley had been overwhelmed by grief, both hers and her children's. It had been a daily struggle to get them to school and herself to her job. Shirley examined the bank's multi-page statements but did not understand them. She'd been putting them in the top drawer of her antique maple desk to deal with later.

Her husband's dearest friend, Neal, was a financial planner. On one of his visits she told him about her confusion over the bank statements.

"Will you look at these for me? I don't know how to read them, so I can't tell you for sure, but I think we're losing money. Where is it invested?"

Neal arranged the statements in chronological order and, coffee in hand, began to read. Thirty minutes

Unsuitable, Inappropriate and Unfit

later he asked, "Has anyone from the bank talked to you about what you need this money to do? How much risk you're comfortable with? College for the kids? Income? Retirement?"

"No, no one. The statement has the name of a man I assume is my trust officer, but I've never talked to him."

"Shirley, may I take these papers for a few days? I'll return them as soon as I'm done."

Neal got in his car and drove immediately to the bank's regional headquarters forty miles away. His discussion with the regional manager could be described as "candid." He was angry because he was a stockbroker and understood the implications of those old statements. What was a mystery to Shirley was an open book to him.

He demanded to know what was happening in Shirley's account and on what basis the trust officer decided to invest in risky securities. He challenged the bank as to why no one interviewed Shirley as to her needs and risk tolerance. Did the trust officer know she had children? Did the trust officer know she needed to augment her salary and the children's Social Security payments with income from the trust? Neal suggested with an innuendo of threat in his voice that, since he was in the state capital already, it would take only a few minutes for him to stop by the bank regulator's office.

The bank finally agreed to reimburse Shirley for all losses she sustained.

The grounds? The investments were unsuitable. Shirley's trust officer, who never talked to her about her goals or risk-tolerance level, was a young college graduate with lots of theories. He didn't even know she had children! His approach to the market, as a young single man at the beginning of a management career, was far too aggressive for Shirley as a mother with two children to put through college and a late start on her clerical career.

A Bit of Financial Wizardry

The number one complaint against stockbrokers is making unsuitable recommendations. The key points NASD looks at when considering a complaint are:
- Does the client have the ability to understand?
If an investor lacks knowledge, experience or mental capacity to comprehend and remember what has been told him, the investment is unsuitable.

- Can the client bear the risk?
  If an investor does not have the financial resources to withstand the loss of the investment or the mental stamina for its volatility, it is unsuitable. This also applies to the technique of investing; i.e., margins, puts, calls, etc.
- Are the client's objectives consistent with the risk?
  If an investor's goals do not match the profile of the investment, it is unsuitable.

12 What's Wrong With Chasing Yesterday's Winner?

"What do you mean nine percent is a good return? If I had been in international mutual funds last year I would have made twenty percent! I'm going to move my account to Big Shot mutual funds, where I can get a better return!"

John was furious. Karen, his advisor, was so startled at his outburst that she was momentarily speechless.

"John, why didn't you let me know you were unhappy? You promised to call me if you had any questions! Changing your investment strategy to growth instead of income needs to be carefully thought out, especially since you are living on your interest and dividends."

John, tanned and wiry from long days outdoors, was in his late sixties, retired from an eight-to-five job, and doing what he loved: raising nursery plants on his own farm. He was healthy, happily married, and usually a quiet-spoken person. His first financial planner retired three years ago, after arranging for her clients to be serviced by Karen.

Karen had been a Certified Financial Planner for twelve years. A plump woman with short, straight dark brown hair, she was a quiet thinker, not effusive or given to exaggeration. She wore minimum accessories with her tailored, almost-manlike suits.

"John," she said, as she recovered from her surprise, "do you remember our first meeting when we reviewed the securities in your portfolio? I asked specifically if your primary purpose was to provide retirement income for you and your spouse. We discussed how much risk you were willing to take. You said you were satisfied and comfortable with your existing portfolio. You did not want to make changes, and you did not want to take more risk. What has changed?

"I remember recommending," she continued, "that we do an annual review to examine your return, look at the market, and update any changes in your profile. You

What's Wrong with Chasing Yesterday's Winner?

told me you had tracked your own investments while working with your first financial planner and would continue to do so. You also promised to call me if you had questions. Obviously something is bothering you and you are checking other investments. Why are you so angry?"

Almost reluctantly John divulged that he had talked to a clerk at the local mutual fund sales office. The clerk showed him historic performance data that illustrated a high one-year performance by their international mutual fund. She also showed him data for other funds, but the one he remembered was the international — with its high return. Comparing its performance to the steady moderate return on his own account made him burn.

"Karen," he said, "I've been thinking about this for quite a while, wondering why you did not put me in international stocks. They're doing very well right now. I'm losing a lot of money at only nine percent, compared to what I could have made at twenty percent. I'm wondering if you left me in the current account because you get a share of the management fee on it. This mutual fund will make me a lot more profit!"

Irritated by John's implied criticism but determined not to show it, Karen said, "John, I would like to meet with you to restrategize. If you really want to have an international position, it should be balanced with your other holdings."

Unsatisfied with Karen's attitude, John moved his investment account without first notifying her about his intention. The following year international was the poorest-performing category, and the strategy he had just abandoned was the star.

But John's reaction was not unusual. Many, many investors, excited by the prospect of increasing their gain on investments, make buying decisions based on which fund performed best in the last month, or the last six months, or one year. Contributing to inappropriate buying decisions are several investment magazines that publish lists of mutual funds under headings such as "The Best Place to Put Your Money Now" and "Top Performers for the Past Three Months."

Buying last year's — or last month's — winner is foolish. So foolish, in fact, that all sales literature, per SEC rules, must state that past performance is no guarantee of future performance!

"But everyone else made money last year: we lost!" was the complaint of a physician who was concerned about building assets for his retirement.

What's Wrong with Chasing Yesterday's Winner?

"At the conference everyone was talking about what a great year it was for them, and we had to admit to losing money. I don't like that. Maybe we should move our money. I have the names of investments our friends are in."

Dr. Fennewick and his wife were visibly concerned about the effect his loss will have on his plans for retirement. In his middle fifties, he wants to retire early, in only six years. After his divorce four years earlier, his financial condition was critical. His only asset was his practice and a very small part of his pension. He was faced with totally rebuilding his financial base.

Happily, his second wife, Betty, was very organized and a conscientious saver. She has had them on a budget that included both an investment program and two nice vacations a year.

Dr. Fennewick's CPA had introduced he and his wife to Baxter, a financial planner. It was Baxter who recommended a professional money manager for the physician's profit-sharing plan, and he met with them semi-annually to review its performance. The portfolio had grown large enough to be diversified between two managers.

Now Baxter was concerned over Dr. Fennewick's anxiety about moving his money. "Dr. Fennewick," he said, "do you remember when we started working together? You told me that you could not afford to take a lot of risk, as you were starting with virtually nothing and would not have time to make up any big losses. We looked at a number of strategies. I showed you historically how many down years would have happened, depending on what the balance was between stocks and bonds. Your profit-sharing plan has performed nicely without taking undue risks. It did have one down year — the first since we started. But I told you that sooner or later that would happen. Last year the indices were either negative or showed very small gains. In other words, most investors lost money last year; you were not alone."

"But I don't like losing at all; let's buy what my friends have."

Baxter paused, trying to formulate an answer that would enable his clients to see the wisdom of adhering to the established long-term goals.

"Dr. Fennewick, we spent weeks developing a personalized strategy. You have confirmed that strategy in our meetings since. The guidelines are that you are a

What's Wrong with Chasing Yesterday's Winner?

conservative investor, have a short horizon to retirement, and do not want to take much risk. Do you want to change your overall strategy because of a single year's lackluster performance?"

There was more discussion. Dr. Fennewick finally decided not to change the investment strategy. He would monitor his portfolio until next meeting.

Six months later, when he and his planner again reviewed his portfolio's performance, it was back in the winner's circle.

An investor named Julian did not have the same good results.

"I thought I was buying a sure thing," Julian complained. "The return he showed me looked great! Now I've lost nearly half of what I invested. I don't know how I'm going to pay my bills!"

Frail and hesitant at nearly eighty years of age, Julian required income to supplement his modest Social Security, especially with his mounting medical bills. He had owned only certificates of deposit (CDs) until his broker showed him a brochure about Good Guy Mutual Fund.

Good Guy had outstanding performance for the past three months, and that was the record Julian's broker stressed when emphasizing the performance data. Unfortunately, Julian's broker chose to ignore the fund's performance in the fifteen months prior to the stellar quarter. Neither did he explain to Julian that Good Guy's value could fluctuate in contrast to his CDs that did not.

Julian bought. After all, he had seen in black and white the return he would be getting. With his limited experience he did not have the slightest inkling his investment could lose money...but it did.

A Bit of Financial Wizardry

Purchases should be made with your personal goals and time lines in mind. To follow blindly, like a lemming over the cliff, what past stock performance has been, good or bad, is a dangerous practice.

Also, studies have revealed that the best performer in one time period is quite often among the bottom performers in the next period. A wise investor's strategy is to find an investment with consistent performance for the past five or ten years. There is still no guarantee, but at least the manager has had an opportunity to test his strategy in several market cycles, and you can compare the fund's performance to others.

13
There Are No Free Lunches — or Seminars

Clarke, a neophyte investor, surprised his financial planner when he announced at a meeting with her that he had made a stock purchase following an investment seminar in which he was intrigued by the opportunity the speaker had described.

"You know, I made this investment," Clarke said to Verna, "but I'm not sure I understand it. I think it was a good idea, and it sounded kind of fun. Maybe you can explain it," he said with a slow, wide grin. He added, "before the divorce Marie handled the investments. She had a better head for those kinds of things.

"I bought this," he said, "because I really liked the speaker. He spent a lot of time explaining the workings

– 105 –

of several investments and seemed real knowledgeable, even though he's only been a broker about a year. I thought this was a good way to thank him. It's the money I was going to invest through you anyway, so it's not like I spent more than I had. Here's the stuff he gave me about it."

Clarke handed Verna a prospectus, a brochure, and his account statement.

Verna, Clarke's gray-haired financial planner, had checked her temptation to blast Clarke for his impulsive buy. She was dismayed that he had thanked a stranger by buying something he did not understand, and when he did not know how it would fit with his already established investment strategy.

Biting her tongue, Verna leafed through the prospectus and the brochure Clarke had handed her.

"Clarke, you bought a unit investment trust consisting of the top ten dividend-paying Dow Jones Industrial stocks. There is nothing wrong with this investment, but how do you know it is right for your plan?"

"Well, a lot of people at the seminar bought this; I wasn't the only one."

Verna laid her gold pen across Clarke's file and pushed a heavy blue coffee mug towards him. She picked up her own and took a sip from her coffee mug before continuing.

"Clarke," she said, "there are two types of seminars: those which are purely educational and those that sell something. Did you go to learn or to buy?"

"Well...to learn. It was supposed to be about investing in the nineties."

"But you bought, Clarke. Let's talk about seminars. If you're going to attend more while you're learning, you need to know what to look out for. Besides having two different purposes, investment seminars can be either good or bad. I'm using good here as in 'teaching investors to make informed decisions by themselves, without being dependent on someone else.'

"Good seminars are taught in easy-to-understand language and provide practical usable information. Bad seminars make you feel stupid or fearful. Some bad ones make you think that a particular instructor is uniquely talented, perhaps even the only person you should trust. Some attendees leave bad seminars feeling they have to invest with the speaker or something horrible will happen to their money.

"There's also a bit of mob psychology used to influence a group. You told me that 'nearly everyone' bought this one investment. That's what I mean: one attendee said yes and others followed suit. Clarke, did the speaker discuss the risk in this unit investment trust? Can you name one of the risks?"

"I didn't hear anything that would have stopped me from buying it, but, no, I can't remember a specific risk in this. Just that it should be held for long term."

"Clarke, many times a seminar speaker glosses over the risk. Even if someone asks, the speaker can pretend not to hear the question. When risk is omitted or minimized, it appears there isn't any! Did you know that at some seminars the only investments discussed are those owned by the sponsoring company? It's pretty obvious the purpose of a seminar like that is to sell. If you don't know any different, you'll think these particular securities are the only ones, or the best ones, available."

"Uh-oh, did I goof?"

"No, I think we can plan around this one. But it could have been much worse. Just remember, don't buy anything without first making sure it fits your plan. You didn't need to buy right then; you could have waited until after you had talked with me."

"You're right. I just got carried away."

There Are No Free Lunches — or Seminars

Investment seminars abound. They are held on investment topics ranging from aardvark to zymology. There are lots on financial topics. Staci, a graying widow, went to a seminar on estate planning.

In her mid-sixties, Staci had retired from her state job as a hospital cook four years earlier. Her piercing brown eyes and dry wit kept people at a distance until she chose to let them come close. She had a son and a daughter, was fiercely independent, and very private about her finances. She had a small securities portfolio from which she was making no withdrawals because she wanted her children to have it one day.

At a meeting with her Certified Financial Planner, Norman, Staci said, "I went to a free seminar on estate planning about two months ago. I saw the announcement in the paper that an attorney would explain how I could protect my estate from losing as much as 40 percent in probate and inheritance expenses. Forty percent! Can you imagine?! There were about twenty of us, and the lawyer explained the dangers of allowing our estates to go through the probate process.

"Also, Norman, as you know, when my mother died there was a bitter family fight over her personal possessions. I don't want that to happen when I'm gone.

No way!

"That's what made me decide to make a living trust. Just knowing that no one can contest how I give my property is a relief. Besides, I'll save a lot in inheritance and probate fees. I even saved on getting the trust done. Because I was at the seminar, the lawyer discounted his fee. I'd have paid much more if I'd waited."

Staci explained, "The lawyer had a financial planner helping everyone list their assets so they could go in the trust, but I told him I already had you to do that.

"Now the only thing left to do is to put my house and investments into the name of the trust. The problem is I'm second-guessing myself. I don't want to take my name off my house. I've been stalling until you could look at this and tell me it's all right. I'll do what you say."

Careful not to show his concern at what Staci had done, Norman asked her, "Did you get your trust because it seemed urgent to do it right away?"

"Well, yes. At my age you never know what could happen."

"Did you talk with your own attorney or any other attorney?"

There Are No Free Lunches — or Seminars   *- 111 -*

"I don't have a personal attorney, but, no, I didn't talk to anyone else, other than the lawyer who taught the seminar."

"Were there any other reasons you bought the trust?"

"Just that everyone else thought it was wonderful. And I wanted to make it easy for my kids to settle my estate."

"Staci, I think we better call an associate of mine, an attorney who does estate planning. I'm concerned whether you have enough assets to make a living trust worthwhile. I know there's lots of publicity about living trusts right now, and they're wonderful in the right situation. I'm just not sure yours is the right situation."

When Norman reached the attorney, he put her on the speaker phone and asked several questions about situations in which a living trust would be appropriate. When he asked the attorney at what net worth someone should consider a living trust, the attorney named a figure far over Staci's net worth. Her assets (house, car, and small securities portfolio) did not have enough value to warrant a living trust. She needed, instead, a well-drafted simple will.

Staci attended a seminar that presented only one

estate planning technique. Its goal was to generate business for the attorney-speaker and for the financial planner who offered to help list Staci's assets. Because she didn't know there were other choices, she took the one presented to her.

Some seminar speakers are wonderful people; others are not. Some are highly regarded in their industry; some are not. How can you know which is which?

Let us consider several different brokers who speak at seminars:

Randy was a tall man with a sprinkling of dramatic gray through his dark hair. Women found him very attractive, which he encouraged. He did an excellent job teaching the seminars his company holds at a local community college. His last session was a free consultation with one of his brokers. That was the real reason he taught. Even though the seminar provided good information, Randy's primary purpose was to generate new clients for his commission-paid brokers.

Randy was working at an architectural firm when he was recruited to the brokerage business more than twenty years ago. He has been featured in the local media; holds a high school diploma; has taken no

There Are No Free Lunches — or Seminars

further educational classes. His brokers, who are all housed at his office, range from beginners to those with long experience. They are paid by commission. Not one is active in their local professional association.

Leroy, also in the business more than twenty years, held seminars at his country club to market to high-end investors and to network with tax preparers and attorneys in the hope of referrals. His college degree was in Business Administration, and he had special training in tax shelters. He had also been featured in local media; was paid by either fee or commission; and was not active in his local professional association.

Leroy's brokers, who were not housed in his office, were experienced; he trained no beginners. If they participate in the seminars he gives, they do it on an equal basis of sharing the work and inviting their own guests. There is no built-in complimentary meeting afterwards. Attendees call him if they want to follow up.

Although there are substantial philosophical and educational differences between Randy and Leroy, those differences will be blurred by the seminar structure. Seminars are specifically designed to impress attendees, starting with the selection of a respectable address. Lighting is important, as are the chair and table arrangement, the printed materials, the refreshments, and the carefully written script. Everything is meticulously choreographed to present each speaker in the best possible light during the time he will be on stage.

Of course, there are speaking opportunities other than seminars, investment planners and stockbrokers appear on radio and television as guest experts.

A Bit of Financial Wizardry

Do not buy anything — well, maybe a book — at a free seminar. Sleep at least one night on it. If it's appropriate for you today, it will be appropriate for you tomorrow, so buy it then.

If someone pressures you by saying, "This is the only time it's available," or "This is the only thing that will work," run, do not walk, to the nearest exit. There are thousands of securities and, therefore, at least dozens of opportunities.

Because someone in the financial services field makes a seminar or a media appearance does not mean he is the best advisor for you. Even if he is well versed on the topic at hand. Even if he has written a book and has been judged to be an expert.

There Are No Free Lunches — or Seminars

Nothing can take the place of competent ongoing advice from someone familiar with your goals, risk tolerance and investments.

14 Follow-the-Leader Investing Can Take You Right Over the Cliff

"My buddy said he was a great broker and had made him a lot of money. I didn't think he would want to mess up his job by nickel-and-diming me out of anything. We were so close that he gave me advice about buying my car, building my house. I just can't believe so much is gone!"

Alonzo looked like the football pro he was, tall and well muscled, with short black hair. He was in his late twenties and at the start of a career that should make him a wealthy person. He was wearing a blue designer suit tailored to show off his broad shoulders and bulging biceps. He sat on the edge of his chair earnestly explaining what happened.

"I'm good at football, but I don't know about stocks and that stuff. I depended on this guy. Besides, it's not like I didn't check on my account. I called him, I went to his office. It had thick carpets and cherrywood paneling; it was nice!

"He showed me on his computer that my million dollars had grown to a million and a half. Said it was all in blue-chip stocks, the backbone of America. I found out later that more than half was in start-up companies and they are more risky.

"Then my broker made some poor choices and did more and more trading trying to make the losses back. He was lying to me to cover up.

And he had margined the account — borrowed on it — to buy even more stocks. I didn't know this at the time; it all came out later. I don't understand why he didn't just follow the blue-chip plan we discussed.

Alonzo sighed. "I realize now I should have read my monthly statements, but I didn't understand them. Besides, I was busy with the football season and planning for my house."

Alonzo's new home, where he lived in the off-season, was in one of the better Atlanta neighborhoods and was exquisitely furnished. "But," he said, "I would

Follow-the-Leader Investing Can Take You Right Over the Cliff

not have built it if I had known about my stock account. The value of my investments wasn't up at all; it was down by 40 percent. I lost $400,000! The guy's in prison, but that doesn't help me.

"I feel really bad about recommending him to some of my teammates. We were all depending on each other to watch this guy. And get this — he wants to write a book when he gets out! He'll make money selling a book about what he did to us!"

Losses because of copycat investing do not happen only to athletes and movie stars. Theirs just happen to be the stories about which we read. There are many other stories we never hear. Copycats are everywhere, even in church, as the following tale of woe indicated:

"I believed if that investment was good enough for my bishop, it was good enough for me. It was supposed to pay for my sons' missions and later help with their college," Nolan sighed. He was talking to his brother about recent newspaper stories.

A sturdy, slow-spoken carpenter in his late forties and more used to working with his hands than buying securities, he was still dressed in his sawdust-frosted work clothes as he waited for dinner to be prepared by his wife. When the meal was served, the parents and their family of six children kneeled by their chairs for evening grace before they ate.

"I've been a member of the Church of Latter Day Saints my whole life and I take very seriously my obligation to send my sons on their church mission after high school. Then there's college after they get back. My investment seemed like the perfect solution."

His children watched quietly as Nolan rubbed callused hands over his thinning blond hair. Their well-scrubbed faces mirrored his somberness. His red-haired eldest daughter comforted her fussy, diapered sister who would rather have had their mother nurse her than in the kitchen cooking.

"All of us bought, you know. That salesman talked to everyone in the Ward after the bishop bought. The bishop is such a wise man...none of us ever dreamed it was just a scam. But our money disappeared with him when he left town a few weeks later. Now we don't have the $10,000 we'd managed to put aside, plus we owe another $10,000 to the bank that I borrowed so I could make a bigger investment.

"They finally caught the guy, but it doesn't help me get my money back. The story's been all over the papers. Made us look like a bunch of fools. He'll get out

*Follow-the-Leader Investing Can Take You – 121 –
Right Over the Cliff*

of prison in a few years free as a bird. I'll still be paying off the bank loan."

Nolan stared into the future as he ran his fingers through his hair. His children gathered protectively around him.

A Bit of Financial Wizardry

The theme in these stories is that a salesman established a relationship with potential investors based on a common relationship with a third party. Because one person invested or endorsed the salesman, they all bought. They copycat, thinking that surely the first person checked it out.

In these stories the copycats are other athletes and other church members. However, copycats are also at country clubs, lodges, health clubs, networking groups, families, and anywhere else people gather.

Sharing a common interest is an introduction. It is not the final word! There are wonderful, and not-so-wonderful, people all around you. You need to be wary.

Do not buy anything until at least your third meeting with the salesperson. You can use the time between meetings to do some checking with your other advisors about the recommended purchases. Check also with your state regulators about complaints and licensing. When you've done all that, trust your instinct, especially if it says "no" or "wait."

15

Bending the Truth About Mutual Funds

Linda, a young blonde woman with her hair coiled tightly into a bun, was speaking from behind a polished oak lectern. A regional representative of the National Association of Securities Dealers (NASD), she looked far too young, in spite of her tailored blue business suit, to have been with NASD for nine years. Her appearance also belied the fact that she was a detective. Her job? To investigate complaints made by investors who believe they have been cheated.

"The second-highest number of complaints we get at NASD," she said, "is about mutual funds. Investors aren't being told about sales commissions, about the new B, C and/or D shares, about internal costs, or about price volatility. Many investors believe that government bond funds are somehow guaranteed against losing value."

Linda's audience was filled with persons who sell investments and who, heaven forbid, may one day have a client call her with a complaint against them. Attendance at Linda's session was required by the attendees' broker/dealer. They hope to prevent trouble before it starts, especially problems that could result in the broker/dealer being investigated for actions of its representatives.

Linda paused to take a sip of ice water from the monogrammed hotel glass sitting on a glass coaster near her papers and said, "With banks coming into the securities arena, many bank customers who have never owned securities are buying mutual funds in the mistaken belief that they are like other bank products; specifically, that they are like Certificates of Deposit (CDs).

"A case I just completed involved an elderly widow who is very cautious with her money. However, as interest rates fell from 8 percent to 6 percent to 5 percent, she found it harder and harder to get by. She commented to her regular bank teller that she certainly hoped interest rates would begin to go back up again. In a few days she heard from a man at the bank who suggested there was another, a better, place for her to put her money. Here's where the stories start to differ.

"She says she was never told the value could go down in the government bond fund she purchased. She says she was told only that it paid a higher rate of interest than what she was making on the CDs and that the government guaranteed it. She also says she was not told there were annual mutual fund expenses. She never paid expenses on her CDs and didn't dream this would be any different.

"The man from the bank says he told her it was a long-term investment. He admitted he did compare it to her CDs, but he maintains he said only that they both need to be held several years. He didn't mention annual expenses because he thought the important thing to her was getting a higher interest rate, which she does with this fund."

Linda gazed out at the audience from over the top of her gold-rimmed reading glasses for several moments, then continued. "The NASD does not care what you 'think' your customer's priority is. We require that you disclose all aspects of an investment and let the client decide importance after they have the facts."

"Yes, you have a question?" Tim's raised hand has been recognized. He recently graduated from college and joined his father's financial planning firm. He was overflowing with the confident arrogance of one who has never slogged through the mud of a collapsing market.

"Ma'am, there are all kinds of comparisons of load versus no-load mutual funds, but my broker-dealer won't allow me to send them to my clients. Why? I don't understand why I can't mail what they have probably already read in the newspaper or in a magazine."

Two older brokers seated nearby nudged each other and smirked as they waited for the whippersnapper to get his attitude adjusted.

"Well, Tim," Linda said, "the SEC wants both positive and negative facts to be imparted. If you are asking someone to buy a security, which you are when you mail an article about it, you must tell him or her what the risks are. The mailing must comply with our rules of disclosure. Media reporters don't have that same responsibility. They write under the First Amendment, not under SEC or NASD regulations. Very,

very few newspaper or magazine articles disclose all the required information.

"Some of the ways the truth is bent is by telling your client, prospective client, or newsletter reader one of the following:

"That nobody who stayed in a mutual fund ten years or more ever lost anything.

"That a no-load fund that doesn't charge you up front will make up for it by charging more per year to manage your money.

"That there's no load on the front end and there's no load on the back end.

"That management fees are all the same.

"As you know, Tim, these statements are misleading because all the facts have not been revealed. People have been in a fund for ten years and still lost money. It is not true that every no-load mutual fund charges higher annual fees. The fund that has no load on either end can have higher management fees than a fund which does, but that is not even mentioned. And, last, it's poppycock to say that management fees for the five thousand or so mutual funds out there are all the same."

Tim nodded his head and fell silent. The two

old timers grinned from the lofty viewpoint of their experience.

"One more case, and then we'll break for lunch," Linda said. "In this one we fined the stockbroker and also suspended her for a time. A complaint was filed by a young business executive who opened a mutual fund account for his children's college savings. He just walked into the brokerage house and was assigned to the on-duty broker. Kind of like the broker *du jour.* A lady broker recommended three mutual funds to balance his portfolio. Each of the funds charged a front-end sales commission. The kids' father set up a monthly automatic deposit from his checking account so he would not forget to make contributions.

"Several months later the broker called her investor and recommended one of the funds be exchanged. She said it had peaked and there was another, more promising, one to which he should move. This went on for several years, with her calling every few months to recommend a change. Sometimes it was one fund, sometimes two. The gullible young man trusted his advisor, so he agreed. However, he changed CPAs, and that was her undoing. His new CPA asked to see the old account statements."

Bending the Truth About Mutual Funds

There was a long pause as Linda allowed the listening brokers to reflect about their own recommendations being scrutinized by a client's CPA or attorney.

"The analyses of his account documents revealed: 1) that there was indeed profit in the account; 2) that her commissions ate up one-third of what the portfolio earned; 3) that income taxes owed on these switches ate up a hefty amount of what was left. Put another way, the broker's client would have earned more than twice as much had she not done the exchanging."

Linda started to leave the lectern, hesitated, then stepped again behind it.

With a lopsided smile she said, "I just remembered that we got a bonus in this case. In our investigation of this broker, we ran across another whose office was just down the hall. He was very excited about selling over $100,000 in mutual funds in one week because it gave him a head start on being top broker of the month. The broker had a lot of his clients invested with a mutual fund manager who did a very good job. Then the manager accepted a position with a brand-new company. When he learned of that, the stockbroker called every one of his clients who had money in the mutual fund the manager had just left.

"The broker convinced them to follow the manager to his new company because of his great track record. The broker didn't tell them they would be in a brand-new fund. He didn't tell them who their old fund had hired as its replacement manager. He recommended the exchange even though his clients would have to pay a commission to get into the new fund. Remember, they had already paid a commission to get into the one he now wanted them to leave! So many of his clients followed his advice that he made $100,000 in sales in one week.

"He was smart about having his clients sign a disclosure statement that they knew about the second commission, but he forgot that brokers cannot use past performance to project future performance. And we got him for that!

"And now in closing, remember, you are the one with the license to lose. You will be held accountable for not making full disclosure."

Tim, the young broker starting out, found himself seated at the same table as the two older brokers who had smirked earlier. One of them, Nigel, had been in practice twelve years, and Galen's experience went back sixteen years.

Bending the Truth About Mutual Funds   *– 131 –*

"So," Tim offered. "You two must have seen a lot of changes since you started."

"Well, yes, we have," replied Galen, happy to parade his long experience. Galen was relaxed in his conference uniform of plaid cotton shirt, tan cotton pants and dark loafers. "When I started there were about 1500 mutual funds, and most load funds charged 8-1/2 percent. Now there are 5,780 funds, and most loads are only 5-3/4 percent."

Nigel chimed in. He was tall and angular, compared to Galen's sturdy roundness, and wore a sport jacket over his powder-blue shirt and tan slacks.

"It wasn't until 1990," he said, "that mutual fund assets reached one trillion. In the six years since then, it's reached more than three trillion — that's a lot of zeroes! I'll tell you something else: there is a lot more information available now than there was ten or twelve years ago to help when you're choosing.

He added in a rapid staccato, "In 1987, Kemper identified a dozen mistakes made by investors when they choose a mutual fund. About thirty-eight million people are mutual fund shareholders, and a lot are still making pretty much those same mistakes — haven't learned a thing! Want to hear what they are? Okay.

- Choosing a short-term fund for long-term goals;
- Choosing a fund entirely by magazine or newspaper ratings;
- Always choosing the fund advertising the highest yield;
- Investing in a taxable fund when a tax-exempt one may provide a person with a higher after-tax return;
- Not having an individual retirement account (IRA) if one is eligible;
- Choosing a fund without understanding all of its charges, fees and expenses;
- Choosing a fund that doesn't have the shareholder privileges you might need — or failing to select those privileges when you open a fund account;
- Failing to reinvest all dividends in order to capitalize on the compounding effect;
- Investing in mutual funds that deduct sales charges from your reinvested dividends;
- Choosing a fund that makes getting your investment out like pulling teeth;
- Choosing a load fund that is not a member of a family of mutual funds; and
- Choosing a fund that is administered and managed by a firm that is here today, but may be gone tomorrow."

Galen put down his fork, wiped his chin, and said, "Yes, and now there is the additional situation with banks offering mutual funds. The example that Linda gave about the lady bank customer whose only investment had been CDs is all too accurate. It wasn't until February 1994 that the four federal banking agencies issued a combined statement to 'provide uniform guidance.' The thrust of the statement was that 'customers for these [investment] products are [to be] clearly and fully informed of the nature and risks associated with these products,' and that 'sales activities involving these investment products should be designed to minimize the possibility of customer confusion and to safeguard the institution from liability under the applicable anti-fraud provisions of the federal securities laws.'

"Among the recommendations were that a brokerage firm operating on the premises of a financial institution be required to disclose that securities products are not insured by FDIC or another applicable deposit insurance; are not deposits or other obligations of the financial institution; are not guaranteed by the financial institution; and are subject to investment risks.

"In December 1995 the SEC added a few recommendations of its own: that brokers cannot use the financial institution's customer lists or other confidential customer financial information to get sales leads without the customer's prior written consent; that bank employees who are not registered brokers should not be involved in offering investment services or receive referral fees for referring customers to the brokerage; and that branches where mutual funds are sold must be registered with the NASD."

Galen finished with one last comment. "The intent of these recommendations is to provide a level playing field for all investors and brokers."

Tim was eating his key lime pie while listening to the older stockbrokers. "I wonder," he said, "what it will be like in another sixteen years or so with computers and global trading markets."

A Bit of Financial Wizardry

There are presently over 5600 mutual funds. The performance of most does not keep up with the market. Some are middle-of-the-pack performers, while others are a roller-coaster ride. A few are consistently wonderful.

Fully half the complaints about mutual funds

charge that they are either unsuitable, the sales charge was not properly explained or that there was general misrepresentation, according to *Registered Representative* magazine's February 1995 issue.

There are at least six independent rating systems which track the historic performance and risk of mutual funds. The information they provide is a great help in choosing a fund that matches your risk tolerance and investment style. The nice thing is that with so much data readily available, you don't have to do all your own research — just apply that already done by others. Check with your library for names and addresses.

16 Prenuptial and Cohabitation Agreements: Before You Jump In with Both Feet

"I didn't even know what a prenuptial agreement was, and besides, if I had, I wouldn't have asked him to sign one. I wasn't thinking about economic partnerships. My God, he loved me! We were going to build a wonderful life together. He would have thought I didn't trust him!"

Charmaine was in her late forties, a blonde woman whose skin was tanned by the desert sun. She wore a red cowboy shirt, blue jeans, black boots, and heavy old silver jewelry. Her blue eyes made direct contact, the laugh lines around them crinkling as she smiled.

"He was one of my clients; I trained his Arabian horse for over four years. Everyone knew he was financially successful. He drove a very expensive car, dressed in three piece suits, wore gold jewelry and ate at the best restaurants. I didn't accept his first dinner invitation, or the second, or even the fifth. I was getting over a divorce — my fourth — and I just didn't want to get near another man. We were just friends, and I liked it that way. He started bringing gifts to my mother, who was living with me. We finally went to dinner and talked about his new mortgage-lending business and plans for showing his horse, things like that. We agreed on so many things, I just naturally thought we agreed about handling our finances. I believe in putting aside something for a rainy day. It turned out he thought it would never rain.

"We got married," Charmaine recollected, "at a darling little wedding chapel a few months later. I remember there were only four corsages left in the refrigerated florist case. Funny how things stick in your mind. I chose the orchid; it seemed so appropriate. Life was great for a year or so. He took care of the money. I trained horses and felt pampered that I didn't have to balance my checkbook every month."

She paused, brushed the dust off her black alligator boots, and then absentmindedly stroked the chunky turquoise bracelet encircling her left wrist.

"I still owed alimony to my ex and just couldn't get caught up on the payments. My husband convinced me that my ex-husband could take my property because I was so far behind. I was afraid of losing it. It's five acres and has both my home and my business on it. The corrals, barn, tack room, arena, etc. Then my husband said he had a solution: I could protect my property by putting him on as co-owner. It seemed like such a simple solution, and I trusted him. After all, he was in the mortgage business and knew about those things, whereas I'm a horse trainer with only a high school education. So I signed him onto it.

"In a few months he told me he wanted to expand his business by opening a second office in another town. At the same time we could remodel our house, especially the room that was my office. He said we could finance both things by borrowing from the equity in my — our — property. I've struggled for years to hang onto my five acres and was nervous about adding debt. He had an answer to that: he could easily repay the loan from the profit on the sale of a house he already had on the market."

Charmaine pulled a cigarette out of a rumpled

package, tapped it on the table, lighted it and took a slow drag. She exhaled, and the smoke curled lazily towards an open window. A second drag, and then she continued.

"He blew the money in poor business decisions and never did open the other office. We divorced about a year later. It was ugly, nasty and expensive. I learned that, according to the law, he really owned half of my five acres. I never thought of it that way, that he was legal owner of half. I was thinking he was only holding it for my safety, not owning it. Things got very complicated because both my business and my home are on it. Our attorneys argued about how much money was borrowed for his business, for my business, and for our personal use. How the money was used made a difference, which was another thing I didn't realize at the time.

"Then I found out he had pulled some shady deals at his mortgage-lending office and violated federal regulations. One day there were federal guys listening in the back of the courtroom during my testimony. His partners also found out about his shenanigans, and they fired him. His federal approval to make mortgage loans was rescinded. In short, he was barred from his profession.

Prenuptial and Cohabitation Agreements
Before You Jump In with Both Feet

"I was trying to get a court order for him to repay the money he'd borrowed to put in his own business by either paying the difference in the new higher mortgage payment or by giving me a lump sum in that amount. I really needed that court order because my doctor says I could be paralyzed if I don't stay off green-broke and problem horses. There are some old back and nerve injuries, so I have to cut down on horse training.

"You know what the court decided? The judge said my husband didn't have a job and that I did, so he didn't have to pay me anything! Now I'm covering the high mortgage and paying my attorney over twenty thousand dollars in fees! My attorney is holding my good jewelry as collateral, a quit claim deed on my property and charging me interest. It will take me years to pay him off!

"The thing that hurts most is wondering if my husband planned all along to steal the equity in my almost-paid-for property. Looking back, it would have been better if I had talked about business like it was business, maybe talked to other people about what he was saying. But I didn't."

Too late Charmaine found out that a prenuptial is a contract that spells out the rights of the parties to each other's assets. Just talking about the individual rights of the partners before they were married would have helped Charmaine define what she expected. It also would have spelled out spousal support and alimony terms. A prenuptial contract can also address the potential impoverishment of one partner, which is where Charmaine is — potential impoverishment.

Stories abound about men taking advantage of women. However, sometimes it is quite the opposite, especially since divorced or widowed men are more likely to remarry within a much shorter time than are women in the same situation. In the rush to the altar bad things happen to good people.

Lorna had a story to tell about how her brother's estate was ransacked by a new wife:

"We didn't even know Hal — that's my brother — was dead until three weeks after he passed away," Lorna said. "None of us were at his funeral. Ellen found out when she called to talk to her grandfather. That second wife just said, 'Well, he was buried three weeks ago.' Ellen was his favorite grandchild; she just about dropped the phone."

Lorna, the sister, was in her mid-eighties. A stroke nearly twenty years before had partially paralyzed her

Prenuptial and Cohabitation Agreements
Before You Jump In with Both Feet

left side. She weighed ninety-three pounds and got around her manufactured home with the help of her housekeeper and a spider cane. Her once-busy social life had shrunk to those friends and family members who came to her, as she could not drive to them. She paused and took a sip of strong black coffee from her transparent flowered porcelain cup, and said, "My brother, Hal, met her when he was so sick in the hospital. She was one of the nurses who took care of him. His first wife — they'd been married over forty years — died the year before. She and I were such friends. We'd all go dancing together. Our kids were born about the same time. After she died, Hal was lonely and scared, too, with getting so sick. When he went home from the hospital she went with him. Just that quick. Nine days in the hospital, and two months later we all drove down to the wedding.

"Then we heard that she caused a big fight between Hal and his only daughter. That was really bad; Hal and his daughter were so close. She took care of him, cooked for him after her mom died. Then suddenly they were estranged, and he was alone with this new young wife.

"His wife cut him off from the rest of the family,

too. She started telling them he was asleep and, at the same time, telling him that his family had abandoned him. He got angry at his family because he believed her. He decided they didn't deserve the things he had promised them. So he gave everything to his second wife, including the jewelry that had been promised to his daughter.

"So many things happened. He sold his own house and used the money to pay off the mortgage on her place. By the time he died, there was nothing left in his name; it had all been spent or transferred into hers."

Lorna stared into the past for several moments, her eyes misting. Then she shook herself and finished the tea in her transparent cup. "I keep wondering why his attorney didn't tell Hal about prenuptial agreements or making a will in anticipation of marriage. Did Hal not know? Did he know and was so sick he didn't care?

"After my husband died, our attorney talked to me about ways I could protect myself if I decided to remarry. One way was a prenuptial agreement; the other was a cohabitation agreement. My attorney explained that a cohabitation agreement is for people who want to share their lives, but are not married. He said a lot of seniors just live together because they can't afford to

*Prenuptial and Cohabitation Agreements
Before You Jump In with Both Feet*

lose pension or Social Security income. Of course, it would work for same-sex couples, too, or anyone else, for that matter. I never found anyone I could love like my husband, so I never followed up on it.

"Hal wanted his things to go to his two children and his grandchildren. It wasn't supposed to happen the way it did. She came into his life and just took it over. Everything, a whole lifetime of things, gone to a stranger."

A Bit of Financial Wizardry

Prenuptial agreements are especially useful in several situations, among them: when one party has substantially more assets than the other, or when each party has assets and each has children whom they want to inherit.

Cohabitation agreements are appropriate for those who plan to live together even though there is no contractual marriage. If unmarried persons have no cohabitation agreement and buy real estate together, it becomes very important to have a written partnership agreement explaining the rights of each.

In both situations, it is necessary to Walk the Talk

after the agreements are signed. Otherwise an "implied agreement" could nullify the original one.

In drafting either agreement each party must have his own attorney to advise of his rights; enough time must be allocated so neither person feels pressured (even if you have to postpone the wedding date), and all current or prospective assets must be divulged. It's also not a bad idea to videotape the signing to show mental and physical status at time of signing.

Bringing up the topic of prenuptial or cohabitation agreements could cause some tense moments. It could also be the positive catalyst for a frank discussion about financial expectations in your new relationship.

What if it causes a broken engagement? Well, you're better off ending the relationship now rather than wishing you had.

Another tool that may be useful in estate planning is either a will in contemplation of divorce or in contemplation of marriage. You do not have to wait until after the deed is done to design your will!

17
Is My Broker In Love With Me or My Money?

"I have absolute confidence in my broker," Lionel said. "I know there are some brokers who are out for themselves, but not mine. I'm a special client, and she calls me only with her very best deals."

Lionel looked intently at his tax preparer from behind half-lens reading glasses. His balding head glistened with perspiration in the glow of the lamp. He waved his plump diamond-adorned hand towards a stack of papers lying in front of him.

"It's not her fault these few things went sour; markets change, you know. It'll get better in a few months. I just need to be patient."

A single man who secretly fantasized about his

broker, Cheri, Lionel did not realize the extent to which his attraction had clouded his judgment. She was easy to talk to and responded promptly when he called, even when she was busy. She also flirted with him. Her telephone calls were the high point of his day.

"Lionel," she would ask, "how is your mother? Did she get over that gall bladder surgery?"

"How did your rafting trip go; are you sunburned?"

"Did the clown get there for your daughter's birthday party?"

Lionel believed that Cheri remembered the details of his life, such as his children, his hobby, and his favorite foods. She didn't; his family and interests were all entered in her database! She could call up the computerized history of his account while Lionel was on the phone.

Routinely when they visited, she scanned the screen for summaries of prior conversations, then wove the information into their current conversation.

Lionel might not have been so complacent about his relationship with Cheri if he knew more about the world in which she worked.

It was one of stiff competition among the brokers

Is My Broker In Love With Me or My Money?

in her firm as they struggled to meet their employer's production quota. Those who fell behind usually disappeared after a few months. Even if she wanted to sell Lionel only her "very best deals," Cheri couldn't afford to.

Cheri earned $182,031 in 1994, which was the median gross income for stockbrokers. Out of that she kept $72,636. Not bad. But she worked fifty to sixty hours every week marketing, cold calling, networking, and selling the approximate nine million dollars in securities needed to net $72,636.

Sales of $9,000,000
x 2% gross commission = $180,000
x 40% commission rate = $72,000 Cheri's income

Lionel believed it was not Cheri's fault some of his stocks lost money, and he planned to buy from her in the future. He believed that she made appropriate recommendations which were somehow sabotaged in the capricious market.

But the number one complaint made to the National Association of Security Dealers is that recommendations are unsuitable. "Unsuitable" includes the broker doing too much trading, the investor not making a profit, the securities being too risky, etc.

The next three most common complaints are misrepresentation (which includes material omission of facts), commission "grabs" (when a broker sells a product because it pays a larger commission than a similar, alternative product), and churning (buying and selling repeatedly to generate commissions).

In the May 1992 issue of *Worth* magazine, Bob, a disillusioned broker with a major brokerage, exposed the daily routine of novice brokers. He said rookies were expected to make at least thirty contacts a day, and that it could take a rookie three hundred calls to find thirty contacts. Out of every thirty contacts, perhaps one would qualify as a prospect; and out of every ten prospects, perhaps one would become a client.

Are you doing the math? That means a new broker makes about three thousand calls for every new client! If the rookie stays on target, he or she would sign on a new client only every ten days.

When Bob finds a client, he does everything he can to hang on to him. That includes, at the very least, making his client feel important. If he doesn't, he knows that another broker, who is also making three hundred calls a day, will try to entice him away.

After watching his fellow brokers for a while, Bob

Is My Broker In Love With Me or My Money? — *151* —

concluded that, "20 percent of the people really care about doing business right. Fifty percent just don't understand the business, and 30 percent are truly malicious. They [the firm] don't care about the clients. All they care is if brokers bring in assets."

Mary Calhoun, quoted in the same article, said, "It's typical for new brokers to be told, 'Tim, I got 10,000 shares of XYZ stock for you to sell today.' The new broker says, 'But I don't like that stock for my clients.' The manager says, 'Tim, you didn't hear me. I said you are selling 10,000 shares of XYZ today!...'"

She went on to say, "We continually see problems with newly trained brokers selling high-risk products — they don't understand the risks, but they need the commission."

Lawrence, a broker, confessed all in mid-1995 when he said, "Each month I started at the bottom with no guaranteed income. Each month I had to build up my gross production and commission...until the 30th day of the month, and then, bang, I was back to the bottom again with everyone else." He described a system in which brokers who do not meet minimum production requirements are fired without warning. In describing the brokerage training process, he wrote, "What I was really learning was manipulation skills. My bottom line was simply how much money I could get other people to invest with me — I didn't care what products I was peddling, or whether the products were any good, let alone any good for those to whom I was selling."

A Bit of Financial Wizardry

Brokers themselves recommend that investors look for someone who has at least five years' experience. That's usually time enough for them to live through a crash in both bonds and equities. It's also long enough to learn the products, to understand the markets, and to have built a reputation that can be checked.

18

Seeing Through the Funhouse Mirror

"I will not have someone ram an insurance policy down my throat just so they can get paid for talking to me!"

Jeremy fairly bristled with anger as he recalled the incident. A very thin man, Jeremy was all angles and elbows topped by an unruly mop of sandy-colored hair. "What peeves me," he said, "was that I went to her for investment advice and suddenly she's pushing an insurance policy. She told me it was the way I could pay for her time. I don't like that! That's why I asked you first thing how you get paid."

"Jeremy, let's talk about the ways people get paid to advise you about investing. Not understanding the motive behind the advice is one way investors get deceived," said Murray, a financial advisor who was also a Registered Investment Advisor and a licensed life, health and variable annuity agent. He had been in practice more than ten years. With a youthful countenance and a disarming, direct way of looking at people, he was a man who inspired confidence.

"It sounds to me as if you need a Registered Investment Advisor, which is the only licensee allowed to charge a fee for preparing a plan. However, I must advise you that since I am also a stockbroker, I will receive a commission on any purchases you make with me based on the plan. Also, I am a licensed insurance agent. If you decide to purchase insurance products through me, I will receive a commission. Do you understand that?"

"I understand," Jeremy said. "For the present I just want some advice and a plan. I'll decide how to implement later."

"That's fine with me. I'll have been paid for my time, so I don't have to try to sell you anything. While we're talking about this, let me just add that, in addition to fees and commissions, there is a third way persons get paid for giving financial advice: by salary, such as is

Seeing Through the Funhouse Mirror — 155 —

paid to bank employees who give advice to customers. There is no direct pressure on a bank's employees to sell bank services or products. However, many banks have internal tracking systems by which employees are rewarded indirectly."

Reassured, Jeremy was beginning to relax and leaned back in his chair. He said, "I appreciate your attitude. Are there many advisors who get paid for planning, or do most need to sell something?"

Murray rummaged through a stack of papers on the floor next to his desk. "I've got a report here that will help shed some light on that. The International Association for Financial Planning's 1994 Survey of Financial Advisors reports that nearly 60 percent of their respondents receive both fee and commission. Of that 60 percent, about two-thirds are Registered Investment Advisors who charge for financial plans. The average fee is eleven hundred sixty dollars and can go up to four thousand dollars, depending on the case. Plans can be more expensive than that; each advisor sets his own scale. The survey implies that it should be easy to find an experienced advisor because over two-thirds have been in practice more than ten years."

Leaning forward, Jeremy asked, "What kinds of

planning do the advisors mostly do?"

"Well, according to the report, the top four services are retirement planning, estate planning, asset allocation, and education planning. There are other services as well, but the ones I mentioned are the most popular."

As Murray laid the report aside, he asked, "Jeremy, how much investing have you done in the stock market? The reason I'm asking is that many people have a distorted view of how it works, and that causes them to make poor decisions."

"Well, I've bought stocks, but mostly through my company."

"Let me give you some broad-brush information. The stock market is a big auction at which investors either buy ownership [stocks] in a company or lend money [bonds] to it. There are a lot of bells and whistles and different kinds of stocks and bonds, but stocks and bonds are the foundation of the marketplace.

"If you lend money through bonds, you're going to want to know the company can pay you back. If you buy ownership and the company does well, the value of your share goes up. The value can also go down; there are lots of reasons that happens. It's important to remember a business's fortunes will fluctuate, and so will its share price. If you've bought a good security, don't panic and sell it at a loss. The key is to monitor your investment regularly, and this is where many investors fail. They'll buy and never look at what they bought again, or they drive themselves to an ulcer by checking the price twice a day. There has to be a happy medium.

"If you invest in the stock market, you must use dollars you will not need for at least three years, and preferably five. The stock market is a long-term commitment. Shorter-term money should go into a savings account or a money market fund, especially if it's needed for something at a certain date. Many people ask where to put money they are going to need in only a few months. It's definitely not in the stock market."

Jeremy interrupted. "Wait, wait. What about the stories of people making a lot of money in only a few months? Why not try to do something like that?"

"Now you're talking risk tolerance, Jeremy. How much volatility can you stand? It takes a very special person with a lot of talent and the ability to weather a lot of ups and downs to do what you're talking about. And very few investors — even professional ones — can do it consistently. On the other hand, the longer you're in the market, the less the average volatility. Besides, you should be in through a whole market cycle to give your strategy time to work.

Murray leaned back in his easy chair and clasped his hands behind his head. "There's another thing that gets amateur investors in trouble. They want to hang onto their losers until the price comes back up to what they paid. That's a fool's game. The professionals know they're going to make poor choices as often as one in four buys. When they buy they've already established a price below which they will sell. The amateur waits and waits and misses wonderful opportunities because he can't admit a mistake. Cut your losses and get on with it."

Jeremy looked at his watch. "Uh oh! I have to leave; my kids have a game I'm supposed to drive them to. Let's sign that contract so I can have a plan."

A Bit of Financial Wizardry:

1. There are three ways that advisors are paid: fee, commission and salary. The method of payment can and often will affect the recommendations you receive.

2. You must have a financial plan against which to measure success and to determine whether or not a specific investment is suitable.
3. You must educate yourself about the market and its advisors.
4. Stock market fluctuations are normal for both stocks and bonds.
5. Short-term investing is a high-risk, volatile venture best left to professionals.
6. Long-term investing (more than three to five years) is more conservative and less volatile. It is the usual avenue for the average investor.
7. Take a page from the professionals. Sell your losers, and get rid of incompetent advisors.

19

Choosing as if Your Retirement Depends on It

"It's the most important financial decision I'll ever make, and I can't do it! I have to tell my company where to send my pension rollover, and I don't understand all this paperwork."

Emery and his wife, Sylvia, were sitting side by side in black leather wingback chairs at his financial advisor's cluttered teak desk. Emery was a small man, dressed in a burgundy sweatsuit, tennis shoes and white socks. His pencil-thin blond mustache was nearly invisible against his pale, round face. Emery paused every few sentences to catch his breath, a result of nervousness. Sylvia was a large woman, sturdily built, with a loud, infectious laugh. Her red-blonde hair was cut in straight bangs and hung just to her shoulders. Her sweatsuit was dove gray, and she had attached a bright red rhinestone pin behind one shoulder, where it floated like a rear brake light.

Sylvia jumped in. "I've been after him for months to take early retirement if his company offered it. It finally did, but now we have to decide where to invest it. All his buddies are telling him what to do, but I'd rather ask you."

"Wait, wait; let's back up a little so I can understand." Howell, an unusually tall man, had propped his elbows on the desk and was peering at Emery and his wife. He had a kind smile and twinkling eyes. His short black beard framed his face and partly hid his prominent ears.

"Emery, tell me about the early retirement option. Your company is offering an incentive if you retire now? One of the choices you have for your pension is to roll it into an Individual Retirement Account (IRA)."

Emery nodded and then said, "Yes, they want me to decide how it should be invested. My employer always handled the investments. I just don't feel qualified, but the company says now I have to be the one to make the choices. They won't recommend one way or

Choosing as if Your Retirement Depends on It

the other. That's why we're here."

Sylvia jumped in. "I keep telling him there's nothing to it. We should just divide it between a Stock Fund, a Bond Fund, and some CDs. That way we'll have all our bases covered. If it doesn't perform we can always change it. Emery is just being too serious about the whole thing."

Howell sat silently for a few moments, watching the interaction between them. It was obvious from Emery's grimace that they'd discussed — and disagreed about — the decision. The large wooden clock on the credenza behind them chimed in the silence. Then Howell began speaking, addressing her first.

"Actually, Sylvia, Emery may not be so wrong in thinking this through carefully. If he's too casual and just invests anywhere, he can make a serious mistake. And, Emery, Sylvia is right; you're not locked into the choices you make now; they can be changed.

Howell continued, "Emery's pension rollover will probably be the largest asset you'll ever own other than the equity in your home. The way it's invested is critical because one percentage point difference in long-term performance can make the difference between a comfortable retirement and a cash-strapped one. You need to develop a plan and to select the most appropriate investments to meet your goals. Now let's take a look at the information you brought."

Emery and Sylvia both reached for the documents in front of them. Emery got to them first and handed them over. As Howell paged through the brochure, they watched. Finally he said, "What we want starts on this page. Here is the list of distribution choices you have and the forms you'll need to sign for your company. You know, your company provided good information. Let's set this aside for now and design your plan."

They huddled for nearly an hour discussing Emery's risk tolerance and retirement needs. Howell drew diagrams and sketches. Sylvia asked questions, and finally Emery began nodding his head in agreement. They had a plan.

Emery asked, "When I get these accounts set up, what comes next?"

"Yes," added Sylvia, "do we see you again?"

Howell smiled to himself; they were cooperating instead of facing off. "Yes, about once a year we should review your portfolio's performance and any changes in your personal situation. You've put together a good strategy; only minor adjustments should be needed.

Choosing as if Your Retirement Depends on It

Many employees do not consult a financial advisor until they're nearly ready to retire. There are more than twenty million workers who direct their pension investments. Many of them also direct where their pension should be rolled when they retire. That means there are a lot of mistakes waiting to happen."

"Well, I always thought the stock market was like gambling; you picked something and maybe it would be lucky," offered Sylvia. "I've learned a lot about why certain investments are selected."

"Me too." Emery was relieved and happy to have the choices behind him. "I've always been afraid of the market; that it would crash the day after I put my money in. After looking at the historic performance numbers, I feel a lot more comfortable about just riding any fluctuation out — as long as we have a long-term plan and can measure how it's doing."

"Well, that makes three of us who feel we did a good night's work," concluded Howell.

A Bit of Financial Wizardry

Most of America's employees are totally unprepared to make any kind of decision for their retirement.

Too few employers provide employees enough information, either in printed material or in personal consultation.

Get help early about investing pension benefits! The difference between getting 10 percent or 11 percent could be the difference between failure or success.

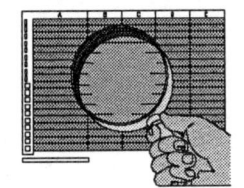

20 Prohibited Acts, Or Is Someone Pulling a Fast One?

There are certain things your Registered Representative (stockbroker) is absolutely forbidden by the NASD to do. A broker who commits one of the Prohibited Acts is subject to fine, temporary or permanent loss of license, and/or a jail term.

1. Acting in a capacity as agent for a client, individual or other entity which could be considered to be in conflict with the employing broker/dealer or any of its policies or procedures.
2. Warranting or guaranteeing the present or future value or price of any security or that any company will attain its own promises, obligations or projections.

3. Agreeing to purchase at some future time or future price any security from a client for his/her account or any account of the employing broker/dealer or any of its affiliates.
4. Raising or agreeing to raise money for any company, individual or venture other than as agent for the employing broker/dealer, without its prior written approval. Such prohibition applies to all securities and to any other investment purported not to be a security. (Also known as "selling away.")
5. Opening any discretionary account without first obtaining approval of a Registered Principal and an authorization from the client.
6. Acting as a personal custodian of securities, executed stock powers, money or other property belonging to a client in their capacity as a Registered Representative.
7. Accepting cash payments of more than $10,000 per year without reporting it.
8. Maintaining a joint account with any client or sharing with any client in any proceeds resulting from a transaction without making disclosure.
9. Issuing or purporting to give legal advice in the capacity of a Registered Representative.

Prohibited Acts — Or, Is Someone Pulling a Fast One – 169 –

10. Accepting an order for the sale of a mutual fund, the proceeds of which are to be reinvested in another mutual fund (except at a nominal transfer fee) without making full disclosure of costs and various classes of shares available.

    A standard industry practice is to require a signed Mutual Fund Switch Form from the client acknowledging that the client wishes to make the change irrespective of the fact that a new commission charge will result and also to require the Registered Representative to notify the customer of any transfer privileges within the same fund group and attempt to dissuade the customer from acting in any way inconsistent with his best interests.

11. Creating excessive activity, sometimes called "churning," in a customer account.

12. Violating any regulations established by the Securities Exchange Commission (SEC), the National Association of Securities Dealers (NASD), the state, the exchange(s), or any other regulatory or self-regulatory bodies to which a Registered Representative of the employing broker/dealer is responsible.

21
SEC and Associations Information

List of Securities Exchange Commission Regional Offices:

1. Northeast
Suite 1300
7 World Trade Center
New York, NY 10048
202/748-8000

Suite 600
73 Fremont St.
Boston, MA 02108-3912
617/424-5900

Suite 500 E
Curtis Center
601 Walnut St.
Philadelphia, PA 19106
215/597-3100

2. Southeast
Suite 200
1401 Brickell Ave.
Miami, FL 33131
305/536-4700

3. Midwest
Suite 1000
3475 Lenox Rd. NE
Atlanta, GA 30326-1232
404/842-7600

Suite 1400
Northwestern Atrium Center
500 W. Madison St.
Chicago, IL 60661-2511
312/353-7390

4. Central
Suite 4800
1801 California St.
Denver, CO 80202-2648
303/391-6800

Suite 1900
801 Cherry St.
Fort Worth, TX 76102
817/334-3821

500 Key Bank Tower
50 S. Main St.
Salt Lake City, UT 84144-1402
801/524-5796

5. Pacific
11th Floor
5670 Wilshire Blvd.
Los Angeles, CA 90036-3648
2134/965-3998

Suite 1100
44 Montgomery St.
San Francisco, CA 94104
415/705-2500

Securities Exchange Commission telephone information system:

The Securities Exchange Commission has a national toll-free telephone number, 1-800-732-0330, through which the general public may access information, including cases currently undergoing investigation or litigation. The extensions are:

Touch tone #1. T+3 (Trade-date plus three days) trading information

Touch tone #2. Information on specific cases under investigation or in litigation

Touch tone #3. Filing an SEC complaint

Touch tone #4. Three public reference rooms, obtaining public records, and the SEC's bulletin board services

Touch tone #5. Disciplinary history of broker/dealers, etc.

At 202/942-8088 and 8090, you'll reach a live person who can assist in filing complaints.

National Association of Securities Dealers (NASD) regional offices:

District 1
San Francisco
525 Market St., Suite 300
San Francisco, CA 94105-2711
415/882-1200
Fax: 415/546-6991

District 2
Los Angeles
300 S. Grand Ave., Ste. 1600
Los Angeles, CA 90071
213/627-2122
Fax: 213/617-3299

District 3
Denver
1401 17th St., Suite 700
Denver, CO 80202
303/298-7234
Fax: 303/292-4272

District 4
Kansas City
12 Wyandotte Plaza
120 W. 12th St., Suite 900
Kansas, MO 64105
816/421-5700
Fax: 816/421-5029

District 5
New Orleans
1100 Poydras St.
Suite 850, Energy Center
New Orleans, LA 70163
504/522-6527
Fax: 504/522-4077

District 6
Dallas
1999 Bryan St., Suite 1450
Olympia & York Tower
Dallas, TX 75201
214/969-7050
Fax: 214/922-0079

SEC and Associations Information – *175* –

District 7
Atlanta
One Securities Ctr., Ste. 500
3490 Piedmont Rd. NE
Atlanta, GA 30305
404/239-6100
Fax: 404/237-9290

District 8
Chicago
10 S. LaSalle St., 20th Fl.
Chicago, IL 60603-1002
312/899-4400
Fax: 312/2366-3025

District 8
Cleveland
Renaissance on Playhouse Sq.
11350 Euclid Ave., Suite 900
Cleveland, OH 44115
216/694-4545
Fax: 216/694-3048

District 9
Philadelphia
1818 Market St., 14th Fl.
Philadelphia, PA
215/665-1180
Fax: 215/496-0434

District 9
Washington, D.C.
1735 K St., NW
Washington, D.C. 20006-1500
202/728-8400
Fax: 202/728-8890

District 10
New York
33 Whitehall St.
New York, NY 10004
212/858-4000
Fax: 212/858-4189

District 11
Boston
260 Franklin St., 16th Fl.
Boston, MA
617/261-0800
Fax: 617/951-2337

The national NASD office is located in Maryland and may be reached at 301/590-6500.

Professional Associations

The ***International Association for Financial Planning*** (IAFP), and the ***Institute of Certified Financial Planners*** (ICFP) are two membership associations for persons in the financial planning field. Members do planning and offer investments. Both have referral programs through which those inquiring about a planner can obtain names of members who have met the program's educational and experience qualifications. Usually several names are provided. In addition, each organization will investigate complaints against its members and take appropriate action, including canceling the offending member's membership. You may write or call:

IAFP
Suite B-300
5775 Glenridge Dr. NE
Atlanta, GA 30328-5364
800/945-IAFP (4237)

ICFP
3801 E. Florida Ave., #708
Denver, CO 80231-4397
800/322-4237

SEC and Associations Information

The IAFP has a Web site (http://www.iafp.org.) with two public sections. The consumer section includes an overview of IAFP, general financial planning information, and details of the financial planning process. It has brochures from IAFP's *Mastering Money* program and interactive forms to help consumers find a financial advisor. It is also connected to IAFP's Consumer Referral Program.

The *Certified Financial Planner Board of Standards* (formerly known as International Board of Certified Financial Planners, or IBCFP) has absolute control of the use of the Certified Financial Planner (CFP) mark. It sets educational and testing standards, annual continuing education requirements, and guidelines for the cancellation of the mark's use. It is not a membership organization; every CFP is automatically subject to its authority. Complaints about a CFP whom you believe has violated its Code of Ethics may be sent to 1600 Lincoln St., Denver, CO 80264.

The *National Association of Personal Financial Advisors* (NAPFA), located in Buffalo Grove, Illinois, is a membership group consisting of fee-only planners who do not sell investments or insurance. Members must agree to be bound by the NAPFA Code of Ethics and Standards of Membership and Affiliation and qualify by experience, training and education. NAPFA has an automated telephone referral system. It will send information on fee-only planning and education about insurance and securities sales people who masquerade as financial planners.

Phone: 800/366-2732.

22

What's In a Title?

---

1. Financial Planner, Financial Consultant, Account Executive, Investment Advisor, Investment Broker, Investment Manager

These are generic terms with no specific licensing or educational requirements. However, several states are considering legislation requiring that persons using the phrases "Consultant," "Advisor," or "Investment Manager" be a Registered Investment Advisor, which *does have* formal state and federal requirements.

2. Certified Financial Planner (CFP)

A mark earned by successfully completing the section, two-year course offered by the College for

Financial Planning in Denver, Colorado. The course covers investments, insurance, estate planning and retirement planning. A CFP is expected to be an advocate for his or her clients, is required to sign a Statement of Ethics, and to complete annual continuing education hours.

3. Chartered Financial Consultant (ChFC)

A designation offered through the American College (Pennsylvania) for insurance agents. Of the ten classes, about half are specifically investment related; the balance apply equally to the Chartered Life Underwriters (CLU) designation. A ChFC must subscribe to a code of ethics, but there are no required continuing education hours unless the agent voluntarily participates in the Professional Achievement and Continuing Education (PACE) program.

4. Registered Investment Advisor

The only entity allowed to charge a fee by the hour. Persons or businesses can be Registered Investment Advisors. There are currently no educational requirements, but registrants must renew each year at both federal and state level and must post a bond.

5. General Securities (Registered) Representative

The industry designation for a person who has passed the Series 7 Test; more usually known as a "Stockbroker." Can offer stocks, bonds, mutual funds, CDs. In addition to the Series 7, there are a total of twenty-five other areas of testing required to offer other types of investments, to supervise others, and/or to solicit clients in states other than one's own.

6. Licensed Life Insurance Agent

The industry designation for a person who has taken the training and passed the test to sell life insurance, including "variable" products that involve an investment in the stock market, hence its "variability." In most states, agents must complete annual continuing education hours to maintain their license. They must apply to, and meet the requirements of, other states to do business as a non-resident agent.

To order additional copies of

Can I Trust You With My Money?
Book: $12.95   Shipping/Handling $3.00

Call BookPartners, Inc.
1-800-895-7323

∞

Noreen Gonce can be contacted for speaking engagements or workshops at:

ProForma Wealth Management
8125 S.W. Nimbus Avenue
Beaverton, Oregon 97008

Fax: 503-626-6915

Phone: 503-626-3700